CAMBRIDGE STUDIES IN PHILOSOPHY

On action

CAMBRIDGE STUDIES IN PHILOSOPHY

General editor SYDNEY SHOEMAKER

Advisory editors J. E. J. ALTHAM, SIMON BLACKBURN,
GILBERT HARMAN, MARTIN HOLLIS, FRANK JACKSON,
JONATHAN LEAR, WILLIAM G. LYCAN, JOHN PERRY,
BARRY STROUD

On action

Carl Ginet
Cornell University

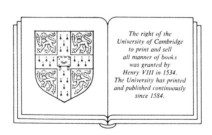

The right of the
University of Cambridge
to print and sell
all manner of books
was granted by
Henry VIII in 1534.
The University has printed
and published continuously
since 1584.

Cambridge University Press

Cambridge

New York   Port Chester   Melbourne   Sydney

Published by the Press Syndicate of the University of Cambridge
The Pitt Building, Trumpington Street, Cambridge CB2 1RP
40 West 20th Street, New York, NY 10011, USA
10 Stamford Road, Oakleigh, Melbourne 3166, Australia

© Cambridge University Press 1990

First published 1990

Printed in the United States of America

Library of Congress Cataloging-in-Publication Data
Ginet, Carl.
On action / Carl Ginet.
p. cm. – (Cambridge studies in philosophy)
Includes bibliographical references.
ISBN 0-521-38124-X. – ISBN 0-521-38818-X (pbk.)
1. Act (Philosophy)   2. Intentionality (Philosophy)   3. Free will
and determinism.   I. Title.   II. Series.
B105.A35G56   1990
128′.4–dc20   89-38039
CIP

British Library Cataloguing in Publication Data
Ginet, Carl
On action. – (Cambridge studies in philosophy).
1. Man. Actions. Human actions – Philosophical
perspectives
I. Title
128′.4

ISBN 0-521-38124-X hard covers
ISBN 0-521-38818-X paperback

For Sally

Contents

Preface

The philosophy of action deals with the notion of action that applies only to beings who have wills. (The words *action* and *act* are, of course, applied to other sorts of entities – we speak of the action of the acid on the metal and of how the pistons act to move the drive shaft – but what *action* and *act* mean in such applications is not a concern here.) We take ourselves, people, to be the paradigms of enwilled agents. That we are beings who act is a fundamental fact about us. It is as important as the fact that we are cognizers, beings who know and believe. (These two aspects are, of course, thoroughly interconnected: The knowledge and beliefs we have and those we want influence our actions, and our actions influence the beliefs we come to have.) Yet, though philosophers in the Western tradition from Socrates on have had much to say about action, it is only in the last three decades or so that the theory of action has come to be thought of as a distinct branch of philosophy, on a par with the theory of knowledge. This may be because there was a tendency to think of action as a subconcern of philosophizing about rationality and morality. And indeed, very important questions about action arise there, such questions as what it is to choose one's actions rationally and what makes it the case that a person is morally responsible for an action. But some fundamental questions about action are prior to those concerned with its moral or prudential dimensions. Just what sort of thing is an action? We like to think of our actions as connected to the past but not made inevitable by it. What must the world be like for our actions to have both of those features? It is this metaphysical sort of question that occupies this book.

Chapter 1 considers what distinguishes the events involving a person that are the person's actions from those that are not actions. Chapter 2 investigates what is necessarily involved in that most important sort of action, voluntary exertion of the body. Chapter 3 considers a further aspect of what sort of thing an action is, namely, how actions are individuated. Chapter 4 tries to figure out what makes an action intentional (which is connected to what makes a person responsible for an action). Chapter 5 examines what is necessary for an agent to have alternative actions open to her. Finally, Chapter 6 investigates what sorts of facts make true a special sort of explanation of an action, a sort that only actions can have, namely, the explanation that the agent did the action for such-and-such reasons.

There are two main thrusts of the book that are likely to be the most controversial. One is the claim (Chapter 1) that actions are marked off from other events by having at their core a mental event possessing an actish phenomenal quality. The plausibility of this claim depends centrally on my volitional account of voluntary bodily exertion (Chapter 2). The other is the claim that freedom of action is incompatible with determinism (Chapter 5). The defense of this thesis against a common objection – that the thesis entails that a free action cannot have an explanation in terms of the agent's motives for it – involves my account of reasons explanation of action (Chapter 6). (Though that account defends the incompatibilist thesis against that objection, it does not imply incompatibilism and is, I hope, independently interesting and plausible.)

Although special terminology introduced in earlier chapters is used in later ones, the chapters are largely independent of one another in that the arguments in one chapter do not assume the conclusions of another. The principal exception is that the account in Chapter 1 of the nature of action in general depends on the account in Chapter 2 of the nature of voluntary exertion of the body.

Chapter 2 is a close descendant of a paper that appeared in a special issue of *Theory and Decision* 20 (1986) edited by Robert Audi. Chapter 6 is a slightly altered version of a paper that appeared in *Philosophical Perspectives*, Vol. IV, edited by James Tomberlin. I thank those editors and the publishers for permission to use that material here.

This book has grown out of several courses and seminars I have given at Cornell over the last ten years or so and a seminar I conducted at the University of Turku in the spring of 1983. I am greatly indebted to students and other attendees in those courses for stimulus and for help in developing my views. I read earlier versions of Chapter 2 to colloquia at Cornell, the University of Helsinki, the

University of Uppsala, and the University of Zagreb. An earlier version of Chapter 1 was presented to the Philosophy Colloquium of King's College, University of London, and an earlier version of Chapter 4 was given as a lecture at University College, London. I am grateful for the help provided by the discussions on all those occasions. I thank Robert Audi, Melvin Belzer, and John Bennett, who each volunteered useful written comments on earlier versions of Chapter 2, and I am indebted to Sylvain Bromberger and Christopher Hughes for very helpful written comments and conversations about an earlier version of Chapter 1 and also to Michael Bratman for useful discussions of earlier versions of Chapters 1, 4, and 6. My thinking on the topic of Chapter 5, the incompatibility of free will and determinism, has been much aided by discussions I have had over the years with Peter van Inwagen, with John Martin Fischer, and with Kadri Vihvelin, and by their written work. To David Widerker I owe a large debt of gratitude for many helpful discussions and for extensive written comments on the penultimate draft of the book, which have saved me from several errors and led me to improve the exposition in numerous places. I thank the readers at Cambridge University Press for several helpful suggestions. I am grateful to Cornell University for a year's sabbatical leave in 1987–8, during which I completed the penultimate draft. During the leave I was a visiting scholar at the Center for the Study of Language and Information at Stanford University in the fall and at the Philosophy Department of King's College, University of London, in the spring. Many thanks to the members and staffs of those institutions for providing academic amenities and cordial hospitality.

Ithaca, New York   C.G.

1

The nature of action

What is it for a person to act? It is easy to give examples. I act when I voluntarily move my limbs, when I open a door, when I speak or write, press keys on the keyboard, slice a melon, or throw a ball, when I mentally say a word or mentally rotate a visual image. But not all events or states of which a person is the subject are actions. There are, for instance, perceptions, sensations, desires, beliefs, feelings, unbidden thoughts, faintings, sneezings, tremblings, reflex actions, and states of passivity.[1] What distinguishes actions from these other sorts of things? What is the mark of action? Answering this question is not so easy.

REFORMULATING THE QUESTION

It is useful to have a standard way of referring (in English) to particular personal events and states, including actions. A suitable form of a singular noun phrase can be derived from any indicative active sentence that predicates of a person some event or state simply by changing the subject to its possessive form and changing the verb to the present participle. Thus the sentences "Sue suffered during the race" and "Tom started the engine five minutes ago" become, respectively, the singular noun phrases "Sue's suffering during the race" and "Tom's starting the engine five minutes ago".

To be the canonical designator I want, such a noun phrase must pick out a particular personal event or state *uniquely*. A designator such as "My feeling a pain in my hand just now" and "Your turning off the heat this morning" may or may not pick out such a particular uniquely. It depends on whether or not I felt just one pain in a hand

---

1 Also among the nonactions are such items as not voting in the election, neglecting to lock the door, omitting to put salt in the batter, and remaining inactive. Such things have been called *negative actions,* largely because they can be the objects of choices and intentions. But they are not actions in the sense I am interested in here.

just now or whether or not there was just one occasion this morning when you turned off the heat. Usually it will be a contingent fact, and not something that follows from the descriptive content of a canonical designator, that just one particular happening or state in the life of the person satisfies it. Usually uniqueness of denotation will not be even contingently achieved without reference to a particular occasion, so I make a temporal index, like "just now" or "this morning", a standard part of a canonical designator. Thus the form of a canonical designator is «S's V-ing at t»,[2] where "S" is to be replaced by a phrase designating a person, "V-ing" is to be replaced by the present participle of a verb phrase "V", and "at t" is to be replaced by a designation of a particular time.

Our question about action can now be formulated in the following way: If «S's V-ing at t» uniquely designates a particular event, then it designates an action if and only if . . . what?

One answer that might be suggested is this: V-ing was something S *did* at t (or S's V-ing at t was S's *doing* something at t). Even if this answer is correct, it is not very informative. But some uses of "do" suggest that it is not even correct. Consider: "What was I doing while my house was being burgled? I was sleeping." "What did I do when I saw that? I fainted." "Then I did something that made everyone laugh. I blushed beet red." Sleeping, fainting, and blushing are not (normally) actions of their subjects, but it appears that our language is willing to treat them as doings. It could be replied that these examples represent sloppy uses of "do", that, for example, the first question could have been correctly answered, "I wasn't *doing* anything, I was sleeping". Such strict or emphatic use of "do" may, perhaps, be tied exclusively to action, but it still needs explicating. We still want to know what it is to *do* something.[3]

---

2 I will use double angle brackets (« and ») in the way Quine's corner quotation marks have been used. That is, a sentence or other expression within double angle brackets is a variable whose values are all the expressions obtainable from the expression within the brackets by substituting permissibly for the individual letter variables in that expression. I will, however, sometimes omit double angle brackets and use a sentence form where strictly I should use that sentence form within the brackets followed by the words "is true". It should be obvious where these things need to be read in.

3 The first chapter of Thomson (1977) has some interesting remarks on "do" and action.

Another answer is that S's V-ing at t was an action if and only if it was caused (in the right sort of way) by a combination of desire, or intention, and belief (of an appropriate sort).[4] The two parenthetical qualifications indicate ways in which this suggestion needs filling out, ways that are not entirely obvious. For instance, the required desire or intention cannot always be simply the desire or intention to V, for S's V-ing at t could have been a completely unwanted and unintentional action. Nor, of course, can S's V-ing at t always be made an action by the mere fact that it was caused by a desire or intention of S's: S's passing out might have been brought about by S's desire to have another drink.

However this view is filled out, it faces difficulties. If the required motive is supposed to precede the action, then counterexamples are easy to come by. Many a time, for example, I have voluntarily crossed my legs for no particular reason. No antecedent motive, no desire or purpose I expected thereby to serve, prompted me to do it. It was an unpremeditated, spontaneous end in itself, but it was an action if anything is. If the view tries to cover this sort of case by allowing that the desire or intention causing the action need not have preceded but may only have accompanied the action, beginning when it did, then counterexamples are not common occurrences but are nevertheless possible, as we shall see shortly.

Even prior to any concern with how well it fits the data, this sort of analysis seems unsatisfactory. According to it, what makes a personal event an action is something *outside* that event (namely, how it was caused). It seems intuitively preferable, other things being equal, to have an account in which the mark of an action is intrinsic to it, in which an event is an action because of what it is in itself.

This is not to deny that there are important connections between the concept of an action and the concept of an explanation of an action in terms of the agent's reasons for doing it. For one thing, it is important that actions, and only actions, can have that sort of explanation. For another thing, a creature can count as an agent, as one who sometimes acts, only if actions explicable by its anteced-

---

4 This sort of analysis is suggested in chapter 3 of Goldman (1970) and at the end of essay 1 in Davidson (1980). Davidson speaks (p. 19) of "states and changes of state in persons which, because they are reasons as well as causes, *constitute* certain events free and intentional actions" (emphasis mine).

ent motives are characteristic of it. It could not be right to regard a number of events having the same subject as all of the actions of that subject if none of those events were actions that the subject did out of certain motives it had, if that subject never acted in order to satisfy its antecedent desires or carry out its antecedent intentions. Such an "agent" is not conceivable. So even if I am right in maintaining that the mark of an action is intrinsic to it, the relevant intrinsic features mark an event as an action only if that event occurs in the right surroundings. The surroundings required are not, however, a matter of how that particular event was caused – not that *it* must have arisen out of the subject's motives – but a matter rather of its having the right sort of entity as its subject. And that is a matter of there being enough events like it in that subject's history that do have that sort of cause (and, one could add, that have some minimal coherence among them and their explanations). This requirement is already taken care of for my analysis by the stipulation that it is an account only of what marks *personal* events as actions, where personal events are those of which persons are the subjects. For nothing can count as a person unless rational agency, acting for reasons, is characteristic of it.

Although it is not necessary for an action to have an explanation in terms of the agent's motives for doing it, it seems fair to say, in light of the conceptual connections that do obtain, that a complete account of the nature of action should include an account of that sort of explanation. I offer one in Chapter 6.

IS TO ACT ALWAYS TO CAUSE SOMETHING?

Another answer to our question of what marks a personal event as an action, which has appealed to many philosophers (for example, R. Chisholm, R. Taylor, Judith Thomson, M. Zimmerman[5]), is this: S's V-ing at t was an action of S's if and only if it was (that is, consisted in) S's causing something. This is an intrinsic account; it is not to be confused with saying that S's V-ing at t was an action if and only if *it* (S's V-ing at t) was caused by S, or with saying that it was an action if and only if it caused something. To act is to cause

5 See Chisholm (1966) and Chisholm (1976a), Taylor (1966), Thomson (1977), and Zimmerman (1984).

4

something: This is appealing, but it is not very informative. We need to know what it is for a person to cause something.

I will consider that question in a moment, but first, I want to dispose of putative counterexamples to the sufficiency of this account, cases where, allegedly, a person causes something but does not thereby or therein engage in any action. Suppose that at a crowded party someone backs into me, causing me to lose my balance and knock over the drink on the table I was standing next to. Didn't *I* knock the drink over? Didn't I cause it to fall over? Yet my doing so was surely no *action* of mine. According to one philosopher,[6] when one hiccups involuntarily one makes, that is, causes, a sound; yet one's hiccuping involuntarily is not an action.

To me, however, these do *not* seem to be genuine examples of a person's causing something. The movement of my body knocked the drink over but, since *I* did not cause that movement, I did not cause its effect, the drink's falling over. Speaking strictly, it is false that *I* knocked over the drink, just as false as it would be if I had been unconscious and someone else had used my arm to knock it over. Similarly with my involuntary hiccuping. Since I do not cause the movements in my body involved in my hiccuping, I do not cause the sound those movements cause, any more than I cause the sound my stomach makes when it "growls".

One could have a different sort of worry about whether causing something is sufficient for acting. One might think that I could, by an action of mine, cause some event so remote from that action that it would be implausible to speak of *my causing that event* as also an *action* of mine. Suppose, for example, that in the course of a walk through a field, I picked up a largish stone and then dropped it a few steps further on. The stone remains where I dropped it, and a year later, another man walking through that field trips over it. It might seem that I, by moving the stone a year earlier, caused this man to trip; yet it seems wrong to add my causing this man to trip to the list of unfortunate actions I have performed. I think the correct response to this worry is to agree that the man's tripping is part of no action of mine but to disagree that I caused his tripping. Insofar as it is wrong to say that one of my actions consisted in my causing his tripping, it is also wrong to say that I caused his tripping. Although

---

6 Davis (1979, p. 5).

my action of moving the stone did contribute to the factors causing him to trip, it was not a sufficiently central or proximate factor – at any rate, not the right sort of factor[7] – to count as the, or a, cause of his tripping, and therefore not such as to make it the case that by that action I caused his tripping.

So far, then, the thesis that action consists in causing something is undamaged. But what is it for a person to cause something? In anything properly described as X's causing something, where X is any sort of enduring thing, a certain structure must be discernible. There must be an event or state of affairs E that is the thing caused, and X must have a relation to E that merits being described as X's causing E. The effect E is only a part and not the whole of what constitutes X's causing E. There must also be a causal relation between X and E.

In many sorts of action – most that we have occasion to talk about – such a structure is easily discerned. In S's opening a door, for example, the caused event is the door's opening. S's relation to that event, in virtue of which S causes it, is S's voluntarily exerting her body in connection with the door in such a way as thereby to cause the door to open.

In such cases, the relation between S and the event E in virtue of which S causes E consists in S's being the subject of another event C (typically a voluntary exertion of S's body) and C's causing E. This imitates the pattern in cases where an *inanimate* object A is said to act upon an object B and cause it to undergo some change ("A tree caused the roof of my car to collapse"). This means that A is the subject of some change that causes the change in B. And it is plausible to think that this must always be what is meant when any enduring thing – even a person – is said to cause a certain event. Let us call this the *event-causation* analysis of "X causes E": X causes E if and only if there is an event C such that X is the subject of C and C causes E.

It is easy to see, however, that this analysis is not sufficient for the case of a person's causing something. For a person S to cause E, it is not enough for S to be the subject of just any sort of event that causes E. When someone else pushes my body and thereby causes

---

7 It would be a far from trivial task, which I will not undertake here, to give an informative account of what makes an action the right sort of factor in causing an event to make it true to say that the agent thereby causes that event. A number of interesting and relevant points are made in Hart and Honore (1959, part I).

it to knock over a vase, I am the subject of my body's motion. But this does not mean that I cause what it causes. For I did not cause *it:* It was not I who moved my body. The person suffering from a seizure is the subject of the events in his brain that cause the spasms of his body, but it is not the case that *he* causes those spasms, for he does not cause those brain events.

What is missing in these cases? Is there a sort of event such that if and only if S is the subject of an event of that sort, and it causes E, then S causes E? We may be tempted to say yes, of course, the sort of event in question – the cause event in a person's causing something – must be an *action* of that person. If we say this, however, then we cannot hold that acting consists in causing something without getting caught in an unfortunate regress. S's causing something always consists in an action of S's causing it, and this action of S's always consists in S's causing something. Given that nothing can cause itself, this entails that every action contains an infinite, beginningless nesting of distinct action–consequence pairs. Although such a thing may not be a logical impossibility, we have no reason to think that it exists in any action, and it is not credible that it should be required in every action.[8] Perhaps there is no event of the sort required by the event-causation analysis; perhaps this analysis does not always apply to a person's causing something.

At any rate, it is clear that at least one of the following three theses must be wrong: (1) the thesis that action consists in causing something, (2) the thesis that the *event*-causation analysis always applies to a *person's* causing something, or (3) the thesis that when a person causes something, the cause event must be an action. (Theses [3] entails thesis [2], but not the converse.) For these three together do yield the unacceptable regress. Some philosophers would have us retain (1) and give up (2) and (3).[9] A person may cause one event by causing another that causes it, but in the basic case, according to these philosophers, a person causes an event E, not in virtue of causing, or being the subject of, another event that causes E, but in virtue of a special causal relation that obtains between the person

8 As Christopher Hughes has pointed out to me, it could be argued that, since any finite temporal interval is infinitely divisible, any volitional activity occupying an interval can be thought of as likewise infinitely divisible. But this argument, even if sound, does not show what is here said to be incredible: that any chunk of volitional activity contains an infinite sequence of action–consequence pairs.
9 See Chisholm (1966) and Taylor (1966, ch. 9).

as such and *E*. This special causal relation – which has been dubbed *agent causation* – is supposed to be sui generis and not reducible to event causation. The relatum on the cause side of agent causation is just *the agent,* brutely and irreducibly. These philosophers would propose, then, that a person *S* causes *E* if and only if either *S* agent causes *E* or *S* causes some other event that causes *E*. One who subscribes to this analysis can hold to thesis (1) without getting into the regress.

But many philosophers will wonder whether we really must posit such a thing as agent causation in order to defend (1). Maybe we could retain (2), as well as (1), and avoid the regress by denying (3), that *S* causes *E* only if an action of *S*'s causes *E*. Can we find a case of *S*'s causing something where that thing is caused by some event (of which *S* is the subject) that is not an action?

It might be thought that voluntary exertion of the body must be such a case. Consider, for example, *S*'s voluntary exertion of force forward with her arm (say, in order to open a door). By *voluntary* here, I mean simply the opposite of *involuntary:* A voluntary exertion of the body is simply an exertion that occurs in the familiar way exertions do when they are experienced as not involuntary, as directly controlled (which does not require that the exertion be antecedently deliberated or *freely* willed or even intentional). Such a voluntary exertion of the body is a clear case of an action. It seems also to be a case of *S*'s causing something, namely, her arm's exerting force. For this could have occurred without its being a case where *S* exerted a force with her arm, without its being exertion *by S*, and this is to say that it could have occurred without being caused by *S*. *S*'s voluntarily exerting force with her arm requires something in addition to the arm's exerting force. It might seem that the additional thing needed cannot be any *action* of *S*'s that causes the arm to exert force. It might seem that there is no such action, that there is no action that is to *S*'s arm's exerting force as is her exerting force with her arm to the door's opening. We will see later that this is not so. But if you thought it was so, and you wanted to hold to theses (1) and (2), what sort of event could you suggest as the nonaction cause in voluntary exertion?

Two candidates seem initially plausible: (a) an occurrent intention or desire that the exertion occur forthwith or (b) an appropriate sort of brain event. The problem with suggestion (a) is that it is possible for a person to exert a limb voluntarily without in any way wanting or intending the exertion to occur. Suppose that S is convinced that her arm is paralyzed; she believes that the motor-neural connections to her arm have been disrupted in such a way that she can make no voluntary exertion at all with it. She might nevertheless *try* (or, as we might better say, *will*) to exert her arm just in order to see what it is like to will an exertion ineffectually, and she might do this while not intending or wanting any such exertion actually to occur, perhaps even while wanting it very much *not* to occur. But it happens that she is completely mistaken about the motor-neural connections to her arm; they are actually in normal working order. To her surprise, when she tries she succeeds: She voluntarily but unintentionally exerts her arm. This shows that the specified sort of desire or intention need not be present in voluntary exertion.

In response to this difficulty, suggestion (a) might be modified to read: The event cause in voluntary exertion is always an occurrent desire or intention to exert, *or to will to exert*, forthwith. But a voluntary exertion could occur in the way just described quite spontaneously, without being preceded or accompanied by any distinct state of desiring or intending even to try (or to will inefficaciously) to exert, and it would still be an action, a purely spontaneous one. Or it is conceivable that a voluntary exertion, unaccompanied and unpreceded by any desire or intention for it, could be caused by external stimulation of the brain. (Such voluntary exertions would be actions of the person, though there would be a point in saying that a person's actions that are externally manipulated in this way are "not really her own" actions.) So neither the original nor the modified version of suggestion (a) gives a correct answer to the question of what could be the nonaction event cause ingredient in voluntary exertion.

Incidentally, the sorts of cases just described provide the counterexamples, promised earlier, to the view that S's V-ing at t was an action if and only if it was caused in the right sort of way by desire or intention, they show that there *need* be no relevant desire or intention, either antecedent or concurrent, that causes a voluntary exertion.

Suggestion (b), that some sort of brain event is the nonaction cause in voluntary exertion, is based on the empirical hypothesis that any voluntary exertion is voluntary in virtue of a specific sort of brain process that causes activation of the motor neurons to the muscles. This hypothesis is, I take it, well supported by now. Someone might object to this suggestion, however, that the event-causation analysis of S's causing an event E makes it a *conceptual* requirement of S's causing E that there be some other event of which S is the subject that causes E. Thus the event cause of a limb's exerting force should be something that would be known to be there by anyone who grasps the concept of a person's causing her limb to exert and knows that the concept applies in her own case. But a brain event does not fill this bill. People who know nothing about how bodily exertions are caused by neural processes are quite justified in their confidence that they cause their body's exertion; but this would not be so if what constitutes the conceptually required cause is a sort of neural event of which they have no inkling. To this objection it might be replied that, if the brain process is identical to a mental process, then subjects who know that they are making voluntary exertions *are* aware of the required event-causes, whether or not they know that these causes are brain events. This reply may succeed in refuting that argument against suggestion (b), but there is still no basis for accepting suggestion (b) unless there is a plausible candidate for this mental process that is not mental *action,* and it is doubtful that there is.

Although the facts about the brain processes specific to voluntary exertion may show that it fits the event-causation analysis, they do not necessarily show that no *action* is the event cause of the body's exertion. In fact, a good case can be made for the contrary. A sort of brain process counts as specific to voluntary exertion in the way required – as involved in causing the body's exertion just when that exertion is voluntary – only if it has the following feature: If such a brain process occurs but, owing to some unusual circumstance, fails to cause the normal exertion, then it must seem to the subject that she has at least tried to make the exertion. (In the special sort of case described earlier, where she neither wanted nor intended to make the exertion, we should perhaps put it this way: She did what would be trying to make it in the normal circumstance of her intending to make it.) But to try to act is to *act*[10] (though it is not

10 This is a proposition that seems to me to be intuitively very hard to deny, even for the case where the trying to exert results in no bodily exertion at all and is therefore just a mental event. But at least one philosopher has denied it. See Zimmerman (1984, pp. 81–2).

In an earlier version of this chapter I had written, "to try is to act". I thank Christopher Hughes for pointing out that this simpler statement is not equivalent to "to try to act is to act", because intentionally *not* acting in a certain way can

necessarily to act in the way one is trying to act): If I try to exert force with my arm, then, even if I fail thereby to exert any force (because of a breakdown in my motor neural system), I nevertheless *do* something in a sense in which merely intending to act is not yet to do anything: I have gone beyond planning to *execution;* I have willfully made a change. So, if there is a sort of brain process specific to voluntary exertion, the occurrence of the brain process is sufficient for the occurrence of action, mental action, in which the subject tries (or wills) to cause her body to exert. If she succeeds, as in the normal case, then she causes the body's exertion by means of this mental action. (Whether this action causes the brain process or is instead identical to or realized in or supervenient on it is a question we need not here address.) Therefore, insofar as suggestion (b) is right about there being a sort of brain process specific to voluntary exertion, it is wrong about this meaning that there is no action cause of the body's exertion.

One can see that voluntary exertion does consist in the subject's causing her body's exertion by means of mental action without relying (as we did in the preceding paragraph) on the hypothesis that there is a special sort of brain-process cause of bodily exertion that makes it voluntary. One can see it by just examining one's experience of voluntary exertion. This is an important point, and I will make the case for it at length in the next chapter.

If voluntary exertion of the body involves the subject's causing her body's exertion by means of mental action, then voluntary exertion is not a kind of action that counters any of theses (1) to (3). The regress does not stop with it. But it does stop with the mental action, the volition, that is the beginning of any voluntary exertion. Such mental action counters thesis (1), that acting always consists in causing something, because it is *simple* mental action, without internal causal structure, and any simple mental act is an exception to the claim that acting consists in causing something.

THE ACTISH PHENOMENAL QUALITY

Consider, for example, a different sort of simple mental act, a sort better recognized than volition: that of mentally saying something,

count as trying not to act in a certain way. For example, intentionally not sending in one's income tax return with payment by April 15 will count as trying not to pay one's income tax if one has appropriate further intentions.

11

for example, the French word *peu*. In speaking of *mental saying,* I refer to a mental occurrence that does not, or need not, cause any activation of the speech organs; one could mentally say *peu* even if one's speech apparatus were totally severed from one's brain. Such a mental act, it seems plain, does not contain within itself two distinct, causally related events, and so it does not have the structure of one event causing another, the structure that is required by the event-causation analysis of a person's causing something. I mean that it is not *conceptually required* to have such a structure, under our concept of it as that kind of mental act; I do not mean to pronounce upon the causal structure of any neural process to which it may turn out to be identical. To see what I mean, contrast mentally saying something with a mental act that does, in its conception, have a causally complex structure – for example, my causing myself to recall someone's name by forming a mental image of him; such an act consists of two distinct, causally related mental occurrences: my forming the image and then the name's occurring to me. But mentally saying *peu* is obviously not like that; it is not a sequence of two mental events, the first causing the second.

When I say a word out loud, there is a mental event, my willing the appropriate exertions of parts of my body, that indirectly causes a second mental event: my having the auditory sense experience involved in my hearing the sound I've produced. It would, I suppose, be possible to rig up a situation in which my willing such exertions of my speech apparatus caused me to have such an auditory experience more directly, without causing any actual exertion of my speech apparatus or any sound. Mentally saying a word is plainly not like that: It does not involve a willing of speech exertions and a resulting auditory experience, or any "fainter" or imagined counterpart of such a sequence of experiences.

Some who wish to cling to the thesis that acting is causing something might venture the suggestion that simple mental acts are cases where we must bring in the notion of agent causation, the notion of a causal relation whose relatum on the cause side is not any event but just the agent as such. But does the agent-causation analysis apply to the simple mental act any better than the event-causation analysis does? For the agent-causation analysis to apply, there must be within the simple mental act an event that is only a part and not the whole of it, an event such that its having the extrinsic agent-causal relation to the agent constitutes the whole act. But there is

12

no such event. The act of mentally saying *peu* is a different sort of mental event from the unbidden occurrence of that word in one's mind (just hearing it in one's "mind's ear" without mentally *saying* it). The unbidden occurrence is not an act. And, most important, the mental act does *not* consist of an event just like the unbidden occurrence *plus* its having a certain extrinsic relation to the subject. Rather, the mental act differs from the passive mental occurrence *intrinsically*. The mental act has what we may call (for lack of a better term) an *actish* phenomenal quality. This is an extremely familiar quality, recognizable in all mental action, whether it be mentally saying, mentally forming an image, or willing to exert force with a part of one's body. The only way I can think of to describe this phenomenal quality is to say such things as "It is as if I directly produce the sound in my 'mind's ear' (or the image in my 'mind's eye', or the volition to exert), as if I directly make it occur, as if I directly determine it" – that is, to use agent-causation talk radically qualified by "as if". This quality is intrinsic to and inseparable from the occurrence of the word in my mind when I mentally say it. It belongs to the manner in which the word occurs in my mind and is not a distinct phenomenon that precedes or accompanies the occurrence of the word. Similarly for the act of forming a mental image.

Still, it might be thought, this actish phenomenal quality may be an impression of a real causal relation – an agent-causal relation – between me and this mental occurrence. The actish quality, being intrinsic to the occurrence, is not itself the extrinsic agent-causal relation, but it is, it might be said, a phenomenal sign of it. This sign could be illusory, but usually it is not. This attempt to save the agent-causation analysis for simple mental acts will not work. For one thing, what makes it the case that the impression is not illusory (when it is not)? What exactly would be missing in a case where the special causal relation to the agent is not really there but merely *seems* to be there, and how would it be possible to know whether or not it is there? Until we have an answer to this question, we have no explication of what agent causation really is.

More decisive is the difficulty, pointed out by C. D. Broad, that if the cause of the mental occurrence is just me, just the enduring entity, and no event at all, then it cannot explain what it needs to explain. A merely enduring thing as cause lacks the features needed to make it capable of explaining the particulars of the mental occurrence. It cannot, for instance, explain its timing. The mere fact that

I was there cannot explain why this mental act occurred just when it did rather than earlier or later, when I was also there. As Broad says:

How could an event possibly be determined to happen at a certain date if its total cause contained no factor to which the notion of date has any application? And how can the notion of date have any application to anything that is not an event? [11]

Yet it is part of the I-directly-make-it-happen phenomenal quality of my mental act that I determine that it occurs precisely then, when it does. It is also part of it that I determine *what* happens: I determine that what I mentally say is *peu* rather than something else. This too cannot be explained simply by my presence then. *I*, simply qua enduring entity and not qua any event of which I am the subject, cannot explain any such particulars of my mental act. This difficulty seems to show something wrong with the very notion of agent causation. This notion takes literally the phrases that it is natural to use in trying to express the actish phenomenal quality, but it seems that this literal interpretation is not really coherent.

The simple mental act presents much the same problem for the thesis that an action is always the subject's *agent*-causing something as it does for the thesis that it is always the subject's *event*-causing something. The simple mental act simply fails to have a sufficiently complex structure. The actish quality of the mental occurrence is enough in itself to make the occurrence a mental *act*. A mental occurrence with that intrinsic quality is ipso facto a mental act. No *extrinsic* relation of that occurrence to its subject or to another event, no relation that the occurrence could have failed to have, is needed to make it a mental act. The simple mental act cannot consist in the subject's either agent-causing or event-causing some event, no matter what relation between the person and that event the agent-causal relation or the event-causal relation is supposed to be, as long as it is something more than merely the person's being the subject of the event.

Since the agent- and event-causation analyses of what it is for a person to cause something are the only ones in the cards, simple mental acts are counterexamples to the thesis that acting is causing. We must look elsewhere for an answer to our question, what is it for a person to act?

11 Broad (1952, p. 215).

14

A fairly straightforward answer suggests itself when we realize that the mental action with which one begins voluntary exertion of the body, volition, is also a causally simple mental action: It does not contain within itself the structure of one mental event causing another, any more than does the mental act of deciding to do something (however causally complex its content may be). (The part of the experience of voluntary exertion that I call volition does *not* include the perceptual part, the seeming to feel the exertion. It is simply the willing or trying to make the exertion.) Since all voluntary exertion begins with volition, all action is or begins with simple mental action; every action that does not involve voluntary exertion of the body must involve a mental action, either simple or complex. Therefore the following proposal seems promising: «S's V-ing at t» designates an action if and only if either (i) it designates a simple mental occurrence that had the actish phenomenal quality or (ii) it designates S's causing something, that is, an event consisting in something's being caused by an action of S's. This definition specifies the class of action-designators inductively. A personal event designator falls under the inductive clause (ii) only if some action falling under the base clause (i) – some mental action having the actish phenomenal quality – has to the personal event designator the ancestral of the following relation (which we may call *causal generation*[12]): Something's being caused by the action designated by x comprises the event designated by y.[13]

There is, however, a problem for the inductive clause of this definition in the following sort of example. Suppose that, while driving, S voluntarily extends her left arm out the window and, by doing this, signals a left turn. «S's signaling at t» clearly designates an action; but it does not fall under clause (i) and it appears that it does not fall under clause (ii) either, for it seems not to have the ances-

---

12 This is the well-known terminology of Goldman (1970, p. 23).
13 Others who have recognized the primacy of mental action in characterizing action in general include Prichard (1949, p. 189) and Hornsby (1980). The primary mental action for Prichard is *willing* to V, and for Hornsby it is *trying* to V. Their conceptions of these actions differ importantly, however, from my conception of volition, which will emerge in Chapter 2. And on their accounts of action in general, these mental actions are not only primary, but all the actions there are, which is another important difference from my account, as will emerge in Chapter 3.

tral of causal generation to anything falling under clause (i). «S's extending her arm at t» fits (ii) all right, since the event it designates consists in S's volition's causing her arm to extend, but S's signaling does not consist in something's being caused by S's extending her arm. If there is something more to the signaling than the arm extending, it is nothing that the latter *causes*. (It is, rather, the existence of a convention that such an action has such a meaning in certain circumstances, plus the existence of those circumstances, plus S's intending of her action that it have that meaning in accordance with that convention; or perhaps the intention alone is enough.[14])

One could try dealing with this example (as, for example, Anscombe and Davidson would[15]) by saying that S's signaling does not consist in anything more than S's extending her arm but is the same action presented under a different description. But this claim is unobvious and controversial. (The issues involved will be discussed in Chapter 3.) It is preferable to revise the inductive clause so that it will cover this sort of case without presupposing that claim.

This can be done by making use of the preposition *by*, which covers both the case where the nonbasic action consists in an action's causing a certain result (as in S's turning off the computer by pulling out the plug) and the case where it consists in an action's being accompanied by a certain circumstance (as in S's voting for the motion by raising her hand just after the chair called for the votes in favor). The preposition *by* also covers another case that we want to cover, where the nonbasic action consists in two or more separate actions of the same agent, as does S's typing *by* by first typing *b* and then typing *y*. The preposition *by* is marvelously handy for our purposes, because its meaning is such that «S V-ed by U-ing» is true only if S's U-ing was involved in S's V-ing in some way such that if S's U-ing was an action, then so was S's V-ing. The only ways of involvement for which this holds, so far as I can discover, are the three ways I have mentioned: S's V-ing consisted in S's U-ing's causing something; S's V-ing consisted in S's U-ing's occurring in a certain circumstance; or S's V-ing *was* S's U-ing, but the designator «S's U-ing» spells out more fully what actions comprised S's V-ing.[16]

14 In the terminology of Goldman (1970, p. 25), S's extending her arm *conventionally* generates rather than causally generates S's action of signaling.
15 Anscombe (1959) and Davidson (1971).
16 It may seem to some that at least one more way of involvement should be added to these three. When I press a certain key on the computer keyboard in order

16

Note that it is not in general the case that the truth of «*S V*-ed by *U*-ing» requires the truth of «*S* intended to *V* by that *U*-ing» (even where *S*'s *V*-ing and *S*'s *U*-ing were actions). It could happen, for example, that one of *S*'s unintentional actions was his severing an underground cable, and another was his *thereby* cutting off telephone service to the whole neighborhood. In some cases where *S*'s *V*-ing by *U*-ing consists in *S*'s *U*-ing's being accompanied by a certain circumstance, that circumstance will be or include *S*'s intending to *V* by that *U*-ing – as in *S*'s voting for the motion by raising her hand just after the chair called for the votes in favor – and perhaps this must be the case when it is in virtue of a *convention* that *S*'s *U*-ing in the appropriate circumstance constitutes *S*'s *V*-ing.

Given the way the preposition "by" works in sentences of the form «*S V*-ed by *U*-ing», we can use it to define a very useful relation between personal-event-designators:

to put a certain character on the screen, I also (let us suppose) activate a certain element in the computer whose activation causes the character to appear on the screen. I can say, "By pressing the key, I activated element *e* in the computer", and also, "By activating element *e*, I put character *c* on the screen"; these uses of *by* reflect the first way of involvement I mentioned, the causal generation way. Now consider this sentence: "By putting character *c* on the screen, I activated element *e* in the computer". Does this reflect a fourth way of involvement, a sort of backward causal generation? I think not: That sentence seems wrong, seems not to report anything that obtained in the case imagined, precisely because the causation was not in the appropriate direction. If instead of *By* we had *In* at the beginning of that sentence ("*In* putting character *c* on the screen, I activated element *e* in the computer"), then the sentence would report truly about the case, but as it stands, it does not.

But, someone may say, suppose that I knew that in putting character *c* on the screen by pressing that key one activates element *e* in the computer, and suppose that I wanted to activate element *e* for some reason other than in order to put character *c* on the screen (perhaps I was testing to see if various elements in the computer were working properly). So we could say that my reason for putting character *c* on the screen was in order to activate element *e* in the computer (I could truthfully give that as my reason were I asked why I put that character on the screen). Here it may seem less wrong to say, "By putting character *c* on the screen, I activated element *e* in the computer", for my *end* in putting the character on the screen was not its appearance there or anything that caused, but something that caused it, the activation of the computer element: I put the character on the screen in order to activate the element, and not the other way around. That explains why someone might be moved to say the sentence in question. It would be to show the direction of the "in order to" relation (which is usually, though not in this case, the same direction as that of the causal generation). But it does not, I think, make that sentence a correct description of even that situation. A correct description would replace *By* with *In*. Note that the sentence "I put the character *c* on the screen in order thereby to activate element *e* in the computer" is clearly wrong; it would be made right by replacing "thereby" with "therein".

17

Given that «S's V-ing at t» and «S's U-ing at $t^\star$» are canonical personal-event-designators,

«S's V-ing at t» BY «S's U-ing at $t^\star$» $=$ def
«S V-ed at t by U-ing at $t^\star$» is true.

(Note that the definiens here can be true only if the time t includes the time $t^\star$.) I will refer to this as the *BY relation*.

Now consider the following revision of our definition of the nature of an action, where the BY relation replaces causal generation in the inductive clause:

Given that «S's V-ing at t» is a canonical personal-event-designator,

«S's V-ing at t» designates an action if and only if either
(i) [as before] or
(ii) there is an action-designator «S's U-ing at $t^\star$», such that «S's V-ing at t» BY «S's U-ing at $t^\star$».

Here a designator falls under the inductive clause (ii) only if it has to some designator falling under the base clause (i) the ancestral of the BY relation. Thus, in the case we were concerned about, «S's signaling at t» designates an action because it has the BY relation to «S's extending her arm at t» (for «S signaled at t by extending her arm at t» is true), which has the BY relation to «S's exerting force with her arm at t», which has the BY relation to the basic action-designator «S's willing to exert force with her arm at t». And the case is covered in the way desired, for the truth that S signaled *by* extending her arm does not imply that the signaling consisted in the arm extending's causing something; nor does it prejudge the question of whether S's signaling and S's extending her arm were the same action under different descriptions. Our revised clause (ii) also covers the cases covered by our original clause (ii), where «S's V-ing at t» was an action-designator because it was causally generated by another action-designator. For in any such case, it will be appropriate to say that S did the one action by doing the other. For instance, if S's turning on a radio consisted in the coming on of the radio being caused by S's pressing a certain button, then S turned on the radio by pressing the button. Our new clause (ii) does apply only to events that are actions. If a personal-event-designator has the BY relation to an action-designator, then it too must designate an action. If S V-ed by acting, then S's V-ing was an action.

We are making progress, but our inductive clause is still not adequate. If the BY relation generates action-designators, then there are two other relations that should be counted as doing so. First, if

18

«*S*'s extending her arm at *t*» designates an action because it has the BY relation to the action-designator «*S*'s exerting force with her arm at *t*», then surely «*S*'s extending her arm at *t* by exerting force with it at *t*» should count as an action-designator. More generally, if «*S*'s *V*-ing at *t*» is an action-designator in virtue of having the BY relation to an action-designator, «*S*'s *U*-ing at *t**», then «*S*'s *V*-ing at *t* by *U*-ing at *t**» is also an action-designator.

Second, if «*S*'s signaling at *t*» has the BY relation to the action-designator «*S*'s extending her arm at *t*» because it has the BY relation to the more inclusive event-designator «*S*'s extending her arm in such-and-such circumstances» (it is true that *S* signaled by extending her arm in appropriate circumstances), then surely this more inclusive designator also designates an action. More generally, if some action-designator has the BY relation to an action-designator, «*S*'s *U*-ing at *t**», because it has the BY relation to the more inclusive event-designator, «*S*'s *U*-ing in circumstance *C* at *t**», then this more inclusive designator also designates an action.

So our inductive clause must allow not only the BY relation but also these two additional relations to be sufficient to generate an action-designator from an action-designator. It must disjoin these three relations. Let us accomplish this by defining what we may call the *GEN relation* (short for the *general generating relation*) as follows:

> Given that «*S*'s *V*-ing at *t*» and «*S*'s *U*-ing at *t**» are canonical personal-event-designators,
> «*S*'s *U*-ing at *t**» GEN «*S*'s *V*-ing at *t*» = def
> (1) «*S*'s *V*-ing at *t*» BY «*S*'s *U*-ing at *t**»,
> (2) «*S*'s *V*-ing at *t*» is of the form «*S*'s *X*-ing at *t* by *U*-ing at *t**»
> or
> (3) «*S*'s *V*-ing at *t*» is of the form «*S*'s *U*-ing at *t** in circumstance *C*», and some personal-event-designator has the BY relation to «*S*'s *U*-ing at *t**» because it has the BY relation to «*S*'s *U*-ing at *t** in circumstance *C*».

Let us revise the inductive clause of our definition by replacing the converse of the BY relation with the GEN relation, so that the clause reads as follows:

> (ii) There is an action-designator «*S*'s *U*-ing at *t**», such that «*S*'s *U*-ing at *t**» GEN «*S*'s *V*-ing at *t*».

We have taken another step in the right direction, but we are still not quite where we want to be. There is one further kind of action that our definition does not yet cover, namely, an action that is a conjunction or aggregate of two or more separate actions. For example, S's typing by at t was composed of two separate actions: S's typing b at t and S's typing y at t. S's rubbing her head while patting her stomach at t was composed of two separate actions: S's rubbing her head at t and S's patting her stomach at t.[17] Let us simply add a second inductive clause to allow for such cases. Then the whole definition is as follows:

> Given that «S's V-ing at t» is a canonical designator of a personal event,
> «S's V-ing at t» designates an action if and only if either
> (i) [as before]
> or (ii) there is an action-designator «S's U-ing at $t^\star$», such that «S U-ing at t» GEN «S's V-ing at $t^\star$»
> or (iii) there were two or more action-designators, «S's $A1$-ing at $t1$» . . . «S's An-ing at tn» such that «S's V-ing at t was an aggregate of S's $A1$-ing at $t1$, . . . , and S's An-ing at tn» is true.

Action-designators that fall under the base clause (i) of this definition can be called *basic* action-designators (even by philosophers who would want to give a different content to the base clause: For them, too, the basic action-designators are those that do *not* fall under either of the nonbase clauses, [ii] and [iii]). And the actions they designate I have been calling basic actions. According to the definition, then, every basic action is a causally simple mental action, and every action has as its basis such a mental action (or is an aggregate of actions having such bases).

On this definition, the only sort of entity that is capable of an action is one with a mind, one capable of experiencing mental events that have the actish phenomenal quality, mental acts (such as volitions to exert the body, mentally saying, forming a mental image, deciding on a plan, and the like). A robot, if it cannot be said to perform such mental actions, cannot be literally said to engage in action. But for some robots, there could be something more or less closely analogous to action. In a human being, a voluntary exertion of the body is or involves a physical process in the agent's body; and this process begins with a brain process that correlates with (or,

---

17 In the terminology of Goldman (1970, p. 28), the aggregate action here results by *compound generation* from the separate simultaneous actions that comprise it. Apparently, the components of a compound action, as Goldman defines it, must be co-temporal. He does allow (p. 45) that a sequence of actions can make up a single action, but it is unclear that his taxonomy has a name for the relation between such a sequence and the actions that make it up.

as a materialist would say, is identical to or constitutes or realizes) the mental action of volition that initiates the voluntary exertion. If a mindless robot were nevertheless sufficiently complex to have internal processes causing exertions of force by its bodily parts that are sufficiently analogous to the internal processes in a human being that are involved in its voluntary exertions, then it would be natural to say of the robot that it acts and even that it has intentions and volitions. But if we still deny that the robot literally has a mind, that any of its internal processes really are (or correlate with) mental processes, then we must deny that it literally engages in actions. We must regard ourselves as applying to it a concept of quasi-action. (And in the same spirit, we might find it natural to apply also concepts of quasi-volition, quasi-intention, quasi-desire, quasi-belief, etc., as we already do with the computers we now use and, as we say, interact with.)

On the definition of an action-designator that I have put forward, *negated* action-designators – that is, event-or-state-of-affairs-designators of the form «S's not V-ing at t» where, had S V-ed at t, «S's V-ing at t» would have been an action-designator – are not ipso facto action-designators. For it will not follow from its being a negated action-designator that some action-designator has the GEN relation to it or that it designates an aggregate of actions. This is as it should be.[18] To be sure, it may be an important fact about an action that S performed at t, one on S's mind at the time, that it was *not* S's speaking to R, so that in choosing the action she did perform, S chose not to speak to R: S quite intentionally did not speak to R. But this is insufficient reason to treat «S's not V-ing at t» as designating an action, either the action S did perform (and S might not have performed any action, might have chosen to be completely inactive) or a special sort of negative action. One might as well say that in choosing to have tea for breakfast instead of my usual coffee, I was choosing to have a special sort of coffee, a "negative coffee".

Though I cannot think of a case where our definition would admit as an action-designator a strictly negated action-designator, our definition does admit some personal-event-designators that combine a (would-be) action-designator with a negative sort of verb. If this morning I *avoided* meeting X by leaving the house early,[19]

---

18 As I suggested in n. 1.
19 "I avoided meeting X" is not equivalent to "I did not meet X". My avoiding meeting X consisted in my leaving early and, as a result of that action, not meet-

and «my leaving the house early this morning» designates an action, then by clause (ii) of our definition «my avoiding meeting X this morning» designates an action. If by smoking yesterday S *failed* to keep her promise, and «S's smoking yesterday» designates an action, then so does «S's failing to keep her promise yesterday». If S refrained from smoking this morning by chewing gum instead and «S's chewing gum this morning» designates an action, then so does «S's refraining from smoking this morning».[20] All this, too, seems to me as it should be.

So far, I am unable to think of any cases that our definition fails to classify correctly by the light of my intuitions. So I tentatively propose it as a general analysis of what action is. It may seem less informative than one might wish, since its base clause refers to the *actish* phenomenal quality and that has been specified only in nonliteral terms. But the best one can do here, it seems, is to try by such "as-if" language to get someone to attend to the right feature of experience, to *point* to it, as it were, but not to describe it literally. The analysis would seem more informative if this could really be done demonstratively: "*that* quality there". In any case, the analysis brings out that what action is can be explained only to someone who in a sense already knows it, who already knows what it is like to act from having acted. The concept of action can be acquired only from the "inside", only from the experience of acting.

ing X. But it is not the case that my not meeting X consisted in my leaving early and, as a result, not meeting X. By the same token, the truth of "By leaving early, I avoided meeting X" does not make it correct to say, "By leaving early, I did not meet X". This last sentence sounds deviant to me, though it might be accepted as a slightly inept way of saying, "By leaving early, I avoided meeting X" or perhaps "Because I left early, I did not meet X".

20 Actually, the sentence "S refrained from smoking this morning by chewing gum instead" looks a bit semantically deviant to me. "S *avoided* smoking this morning by chewing gum instead" seems a more apt way to express the thought.

2

Voluntary exertion of the body

The action of opening a door consists in the agent's voluntarily exerting parts of her body – her arm and hand, let us suppose – in such a way that that action (the voluntary exertion of the body) causes the door to open.[1] It is possible, in principle, to open a door without using any voluntary exertion to do so. Conceivably, a person's brain could be so wired to a door that merely by mentally saying "Open sesame!", and without any exertion of her body, she could cause the door to open. There are ways in which one can act on or with one's body without engaging in any voluntary exertion. (For example, sexual arousal can be produced by forming appropriate mental images.) And our lives are filled with *mental* actions – mentally saying things, forming mental images, and the like – that, though they may affect the body, do not in themselves and in virtue of their very notion include any bodily event, whether voluntary exertion or other. But it is nonetheless true that actions done by voluntarily exerting the body, together with voluntary exertions themselves, comprise most of the actions that we have occasion to consider explicitly. Our voluntary exertions of our bodies are a central and especially important sort of action. We must understand what they are if we are to understand most sorts of actions we talk about.

PICKING OUT VOLITION

The action of opening a door is composed of another action – a voluntary exertion of the body – plus its causing a certain result. Is the voluntary exertion – say, the agent's exerting force forward with her arm – similarly composed, of an action producing a result?

---

1 Recall that by *voluntary* I mean simply the negation of *involuntary*. A voluntary exertion is one that occurs in the familiar way exertions do when they are experienced as not involuntary, as directly controlled, whether or not they are deliberated or *freely* willed or even intentional.

23

There is a clear candidate here for the role of the result, namely, the arm's exerting force. The arm could have exerted exactly the same force, by means of just the same muscle contractions, *without* the agent's voluntarily exerting the force with the arm. So the exerting of force by the arm is only a part of the whole action. But does the remainder consist of this part's being caused by action of the agent's? Yes, as I indicated in Chapter 1, contrary to the view of many philosophers of action, it does.

The remainder consists in the body's exertion's being caused by a certain sort of *mental* activity, a sort that philosophers and psychologists of old called *volition*. This mental activity is, in C. S. Peirce's words, one of those "kinds of phenomena with which every man's experience is so saturated that he usually pays no particular attention to them". We may fail to notice it at all.[2] The focus of our interest almost always lies in the body's exertion and its intended result (getting the door open). It almost never happens that this focus is disturbed, and transferred inward to our volition, by our volition's failing to produce the willed bodily exertion. Volition is very reliable. And we seldom have any other reason to pay attention to our volition as such. So it is easy to be blind to it.[3] But volition can be noticed, and without great difficulty, if you know where to look.

The first point to note is that when we voluntarily exert parts of our bodies, we *experience* this exertion and we experience it *as voluntary*. We experience the specific exertions that we make voluntarily, and it is part of this experience that the exertions seem to us to be ones that we *control* in a quite direct way.

This is most clear, perhaps, in those cases of voluntary exertion where we have to concentrate on what we are doing with the body. Compare my experience of trying an unfamiliar dance movement with my left leg with my experience of taking a step with that leg in the course of walking along and thinking about philosophy. There is a large difference. In the first case, my attention is focused on my

2 Wittgenstein (1958, I:129) speaks of "aspects of things" that "are hidden because of their simplicity and familiarity. (One is unable to notice something because it is always before one's eyes)." These words apply aptly to volition, but I do not suppose that it is one of the things Wittgenstein had in mind.

3 In recent decades, there has been a trend among philosophers to deny volition. This seems to have been a hangover from the excesses of philosophical behaviorism. In the rejection of introspectionist psychology and the older philosophy of mind, volition was one of the babies thrown out with the bathwater (subjective sense experience in perception was another one).

exertion with the leg. I note just how I am trying to exert it and just how the exertion I produce feels. But in the second case, I do not attend at all to my exertion with the leg. I do it, as we say, "automatically", without having to think about it at all in order to get the leg exertion I want. I do not note even that I am now exerting a leg, much less just what that particular exertion feels like. But, great as the difference between these cases is, it should not be exaggerated. It is nothing like the difference between one of them and an exertion of my muscles that I do not experience at all, such as (most of the time) the exertions of my heart muscles or my intestines. Even when I walk "automatically", without thinking about it, there is a way in which I experience my exerting my legs, a way in which I am at the time aware of doing what I do with them, that is a way I do *not* usually experience at all, am not usually aware at all, of my intestine's exertions.

And this experience of *voluntarily* exerting my legs, even when most "automatic", also differs radically from the occasional experience I have of exertions by parts of my body that I do not voluntarily control. Occasionally I *am* aware of my heart's beating or of peristaltic movements of my digestive organs. In these cases, though I experience the organ's exertions, I do not experience them as ones that I voluntarily determine, as ones of which I am the agent. I experience them as ones that happen whether I will them or not, as ones of which I am only a patient. But with *voluntary* exertions, my awareness of them as I make them, even when it is of the most non-attentive sort, is colored with this aspect of their being *my* exertions, ones I make and control: It is *actish* in its phenomenal quality.[4]

And I experience my voluntary exertions as the *specific* exertions they are – at least in those respects that I voluntarily determine. If in the course of walking I had made an appreciably different movement with my leg at one point than the one I actually made – taking a much longer step, say, than the one I actually took – my experience of making the movement would have been correspondingly different, whether or not I was attending to making the movement.

---

4 With respect to my occasional awareness of the exertions of my intestines or heart muscles, there is the further difference that what I am directly aware of is not the contracting and relaxing of the muscles themselves but rather certain consequences of those muscular exertions. Direct awareness of involuntary muscular exertion occurs in cases of muscular exertions that are typically voluntary but that can also occur involuntarily, as in the reflex kicking response to a sharp tap on the knee.

All this is clear enough, I think, when we are talking about such voluntary exertions as are involved in walking or dancing or pushing a door open. But what about the much subtler ones involved in, say, talking or singing? In vocalizing I voluntarily control exertions by my lips, jaw, tongue, parts of my throat, and the muscles that force expulsion of air through the vocal cords. I voluntarily do various subtly different things with all of these bodily parts in order to produce the many different features of pitch, volume, tone quality, and so on that I intentionally produce in my vocal sounds. It may be thought implausible to suggest that I am aware at all of *these* things I do. All I *think* of while I speak are the kinds of sounds I aim to produce, or perhaps something more abstract than that. The specific bodily mechanics of their production are, it might be said, something of which I am completely unaware.

Well, this must be a bit of an exaggeration. The bodily mechanics may be something to which I am usually quite *oblivious* but, if they are voluntary, they cannot be something of which I am, literally, completely unaware. They are not, for example, like those exertions of my heart or digestive muscles of which I am completely unaware. I am unquestionably aware in some way of using my mouth and throat in particular ways in order to produce my vocal sounds. It is not as if I mentally command the production of a certain sound and lo! it is there, but I have no intimation at all of what my body does to produce it. Voluntarily to use one's mouth and throat to speak is to be more experientially engaged with those bodily parts than that. That other, unheard of way of producing sounds would seem radically different from normal vocalizing partly because I would not *experience* doing things with those bodily parts.

But, it may be asked, do I experience all the specific differences of the subtly different things I voluntarily do in order to make the different sounds – for example, the different thing I do with my lips in order to sound *eee* rather than *ooo*, the different thing I do with my tongue in order to say *though* rather than *toe,* or the different thing I do in my throat to make the pitch go higher rather than lower? If I am asked to *describe* what I do, I am likely to be at a loss, but then there are many features of my experience that I cannot put into words. And if I ever do become able to say what I do, it will not be until after I *notice* what I do.

And the latter, of course, I can do. I can attend to what I experience when I utter certain sounds, attend to just how I hold or move my tongue and lips, how I tighten or thrust up in my throat, and so on. What am I doing when I *attend* to these things? Is it like looking at something I am doing that I do not normally look at in order to find out how it looks? Do I train on those parts of my body some perceptual faculty, some means of experiencing them, that I do not normally train on them, in order to gain a new sort of experience of my speaking that I have not had before? Obviously it is not like that. Rather, I focus attention on an aspect of my experience that was always there but was unattended. It is like paying attention to the pain I have been feeling in order to be sure whether or not it has moved slightly, or like making myself notice the color of the wall I have been staring at while lost in thought.

Consider this: It makes sense to hope that someone who has just watched a person pass in front of her will be able to recall the color of that person's clothing, even though the viewer was not making any special effort to notice that aspect of what she was seeing. Similarly, it makes sense to hope that someone who has just finished vocalizing the word *thistle,* but without having set herself to notice what she did with her tongue, will nevertheless be able to recall what she did with it if she is asked soon enough afterward. In either case, the hope makes sense only on the assumption that what it is hoped the person will be able to recall is something she *experienced* at the time it happened. Or again, it is natural to expect that someone who sings but has never paid attention to what he does in his throat in order to raise the pitch of a note will be able to comply straightaway with the following request: "While making no sound at all, do what you do in your throat when you raise the pitch of a note you are singing". This expectation betrays a belief that such a person must have all along been aware in some way of what he was voluntarily doing in his throat in order to raise the pitch.

So the first point is that whenever we voluntarily exert our bodies, we experience this exertion as voluntary exertion of the definite sort that we voluntarily determine it to be. This does not mean that we notice the sort we experience it as or, even if we notice it, that we are able to describe it.

The next point to note is this: It is conceivable that, at a time when I am actually making no voluntary exertion of my body, when it is quite inert, it should nevertheless *seem* to me that I am voluntarily exerting it in some familiar way. It might seem to me that I am voluntarily exerting my legs as in walking, or my arm and hand as

27

in opening a door, or my vocal apparatus as in talking, and it might seem so to me in just the way it does when I am actually doing it. Our experience of our voluntary exertion is a *mental* process that is separate from – and could exist in the absence of – any bodily exertion.

The final point to note is that the normal subjective experience of voluntarily exerting the body in a certain way is a compound of two importantly different parts. There is, first of all, a *perceptual* aspect: One perceives the exertion in a certain direct way – not visually or by feeling it with some other part of one's body, but *kinesthetically*. You would directly feel the bodily part exerting force even if you did not see it or bring any other part of your body into contact with it. And you would directly feel it in the same way even if it occurred *in*voluntarily. The experience of *voluntary* exertion is significantly more than the mere kinesthetic perception of the exertion. I could kinesthetically feel my arm exerting force, in just the same way it does when I voluntarily thrust it forward, without experiencing this exertion as something I control, as my voluntary doing. I could experience it as something that just happens to me, unconnected with my will, while at the same time experiencing the exertion of the bodily part as just like one I might have produced voluntarily. The voluntariness of the experience of voluntary exertion is a *further* part of it, distinct from the perceptual part, an aspect that would be more conspicuous by its absence than it is by its presence.

It is, of course, this nonperceptual part that is the volitional part of the experience. This part too could occur all by itself, unaccompanied by any perception of exertion. It could seem to me that I voluntarily exert a force forward with my arm without at the same time its seeming to me that I *feel* the exertion happening: The arm feels kinesthetically anesthetized. (Sometimes, after an injection of anesthetic at the dentist's office, my tongue seems to me thus kinesthetically dead as I voluntarily exercise it: I then have an illusion that my will fails to engage my tongue.)

Neither sort of impoverished experience – the seeming to feel an exertion without seeming voluntarily to make it, or the seeming voluntarily to make it without seeming to feel it – happens very often or is easy to make happen. But both are easy to imagine. Both do in fact occasionally occur. And we know enough about how our experience depends on what happens in our neural system to know how it is possible in principle to produce either sort. We know how seeming to make an exertion without seeming to feel it could be produced, for we know that our *efferent* neural capacity to make a given sort of voluntary exertion (the capacity for neuro-motor output from the brain) could be left unimpaired while we were deprived of the *afferent* neural capacity to perceive the exertion (the capacity for kinesthetic neural input to the brain).[5] And we know how seeming to feel a given sort of exertion could occur without its seeming voluntary, for we know that the same *afferent* neural input that produces a subject's experience of seeming to feel a bodily exertion when he is voluntarily making it could in principle be produced by sources outside his body when he was not actually trying to make any exertion.

So the mental action I mean by volition is an aspect, a constituent, of its seeming to one that one voluntarily exerts the body. One will not find volition if one looks for it among the *antecedents* of the experience of voluntary exertion itself, if one supposes it to be a prior mental occurrence that triggers the whole package of the exertion and the experience of it – as I suspect many do who fail to find it. Volition does not precede the experience of voluntarily exerting but is a part of it.[6] It is the part whose presence is what makes the exertion seem voluntary and whose subtraction from the experience would make the exertion seem *in*voluntary, would make it seem that one's body exerts "on its own" without benefit of one's voluntary control.

5 This is not to deny that our capacity voluntarily to make a certain sort of exertion might, in some cases, depend on our having perceived *prior* exertions. A certain sort of exertion might be a stage in a sequence of exertions that is such that we are unable to produce this stage unless we have produced *and perceived* the earlier stages.

6 Searle (1983), ch. 3, although wishing to have no truck with volition, gives to something he calls *intention in action* a role similar to the one I give to volition in that it is the initial *part,* rather than a cause or accompaniment, of action.

   As I remarked in a note to Chapter 1, the *willings* of Prichard (1949) and the *tryings* of Hornsby (1980) play somewhat the same role in their accounts of action as volitions play in my account. Their terms designate mental actions that would be basic and the initial parts of nonbasic actions were it not for the fact that neither Prichard nor Hornsby countenances nonbasic actions (they are what in Chapter 3 I term *minimizers* with respect to the individuation of action). But neither of their terms designates the kind of mental activity I am calling *volition* (note 9 of this chapter explains why not).

Assuming that I have indicated sufficiently well the part of experience that I mean by volition, I now wish to consider its nature more closely. It is appropriate to characterize this volitional part of the experience of voluntary exertion as mental *action*. Suppose that this part of the experience did occur by itself, unaccompanied by perception of the exertion. Suppose that the reason is that there is no exertion. This would happen if my arm suddenly became paralyzed, without any sign of this to me, and I tried to exert force with it. In that case, my trying to exert would consist only in the nonperceptual volitional experience. Since I am unaware of the paralysis, I might mistakenly think that I actually was exerting with my arm. But I would *correctly* think, I would *know*, that I was at least trying to exert with it. I could hardly be mistaken about that, and this is because my having this volitional experience, of which I am directly aware, *counts* in these circumstances as my trying to exert with it. And whatever counts as trying to act counts as acting.

Whether or not an experience of bodily exertion is one in which the exertion *seems voluntary* is precisely a matter of whether or not there is in it this mental action I am calling volition. And volition is essential not only to an exertion's *seeming* voluntary but also to its *being* voluntary. If I voluntarily exert my body, then it must seem to me that I do so voluntarily; if, on the other hand, my body exerts and it *seems* to me to do this without benefit of my voluntary control, then it *does* do this without benefit of my voluntary control. Nothing can count as my voluntarily exerting my body if it does not seem to me at the time that my body's exertion is in virtue of my voluntary control of it. Volition is conceptually necessary to voluntary bodily exertion.

The mental act of volition is *simple:* It does not contain within itself the structure of a mental act causing another mental occurrence. (Remember that the part of the experience of seeming to exert voluntarily that I am calling volition does *not* include the perceptual part, the seeming to feel the exertion. The latter part is caused by the volitional part, indirectly, through causing the exertion itself.) Volition is the initial part or stage of voluntary exertion (and thereby of any action that involves voluntary exertion, such as opening a door or waving goodbye or saying "hello"). It is the means by which I cause my body's exertion when I voluntarily exert it. For my volition counts as my trying to exert it, that is, as my trying to cause it to exert. So when I succeed, it is by this trying, this volition, that I cause it.

If there is a specific sort of brain process involved in voluntary exertion that occurs when and only when the subject at least tries to exert (that is, has an experience of its seeming as if she voluntarily exerts) – as I suppose is now known to be the case – then this sort of brain process occurs when and only when volition occurs. The one sort of occurrence is necessary and sufficient for the other. This can be accepted without yet taking any position on the metaphysical question of the relation between mind and body. A materialist will naturally take the volition to be identical to the brain process (or some initial part of it); a dualist will suppose that the volition causes the brain process. I intend the account of volition and voluntary exertion I give here to leave open the question of which of these views is correct.

THE CONTENT OF VOLITION

Volitional activity resembles various other sorts of mental activities and states in having *intentional content*. The volition involved in my voluntarily exerting a certain force with my arm is volition to exert that sort of force. Whether or not it actually produces the exertion, its being a volition to exert a certain force is an intrinsic property of the mental activity itself, in the same way that it is an intrinsic property of a certain belief of mine that it is a belief that I am exerting my arm.

It is customary to ascribe mental acts and states having intentional content by using an appropriate verb (for example, *believes, intends, hopes, desires, wishes*) followed by a "that" clause that expresses the proposition that is the content of that particular mental state or act. I wish to follow this practice in talking about volition, but unfortunately there is no verb of English that stands to *volition,* as I use this term, in the way that *intends* stands to *intention. Wills* comes as close as any, but it has a much broader use than just to ascribe the sort of thing I am calling volition. It is sometimes so used that in merely having decided to buy a microcomputer, or in merely wanting to have one, I will that I have one; and in such a case, what I will includes events or states of affairs outside my body. But the special sort of mental process I am calling volition is not intending or desiring to do something but trying to do it, and its content or object does not go beyond exerting force with one's body in the immediate present. So the forms "S wills that . . ." and "S wills to . . ." are not entirely satisfactory for ascribing volitions. They are, nevertheless, the forms I am going to use, with the stipulation that in my use of them the verb *wills* is to be taken in a special, artificial sense restricted to the mental activity I have singled out.

Volition is a species of occurrent mental process having intentional content. Occurrent desire and occurrent intention are *other* species of the same genus. Volition is not a kind of occurrent desire.[7] For one thing, volition is action, and no desire, not even occurrent desire, is action. For another thing, as we noted in Chapter 1, it is possible to have volition to exert the body in a certain way without at the time in any way desiring or intending to exert it in that way. This would happen, for example, if I were sure that my arm is paralyzed and I tried to exert it just to see what it is like to will exertion inefficaciously but not wanting at all to exert it. (Suppose that this happens while I am acting a part in which I have just died and am lying inert on the stage: I want very much that my arm *not* exert any force and firmly intend to do nothing that would have that result.) If I were mistaken about my arm's being paralyzed, I would exert it voluntarily but not intentionally. This shows also that volition is not a species of decision or occurrent intention.[8]

Volition differs from deciding also in not being a single-shot mental act with a static content. Volition is a fluid mental activity whose content is continually changing; at each moment, it is concerned only with bodily exertion in the immediate present. I can all at one time decide to swim another length of the pool, but I cannot all at one time *will* the whole sequence of bodily exertions involved in

7 Contrary to what is maintained in Goldman (1976, pp. 67–84).
8 Contrary to what is maintained in Sellars (1976, pp. 47–66). Bratman (1987, p.130) makes the point that, if volition to V is equated with trying or attempting or endeavoring to V, then it does not imply intending to V. But his reasons (which I will explain in Chapter 4) are very different from those I give here. The case I consider, unlike those that Bratman considers, seems to be one where it is not quite literally correct to use *tried* in reporting the volition (hence my italicizing the word). This is connected with the fact that on my use of *volition* the content of one's volition must be at this moment to exert a certain force with a certain part of one's body; but in the use of *volition* that Bratman considers, there is no such restriction on a volition's content: A volition's content may range as widely as that of an intention.

swimming another length, any more than I can *perform* that sequence of exertions all at one time. Indeed, I cannot all at one instant will the whole sequence of exertions involved in just taking one more complete stroke with my right arm. Volition is part of the experience of voluntary exertion, and its content, unlike the content of a decision or intention, is as much tied to the immediate present as is voluntary exertion itself.

As we approach an instant, the content of volitional activity approaches an unchanging, frozen proposition about the immediate present. What is the content of such a proposition? I have already spoken of the exertion of force by a part of the body. What I will at a particular moment is to exert at that moment a certain more or less determinate degree of force in a certain more or less determinate direction with one or more parts of my body. I do not will to *move* my body. The content of volition is not concerned with movement, only with exertion of directed force at the moment (a momentary force vector). Of course, one often wills to exert a certain directed force with a certain bodily part in order to move that part. When, for example, I move a lever, I will to exert force in a certain direction with my arm that grasps the lever and keep on so willing for a fraction of a second, and I do this in order to carry out my intention of moving my arm a certain distance and thereby moving the lever a certain distance. But on another occasion I might engage in the very same sort of volition, willing to exert the same force in the same direction with the same arm against the same lever, not with the intention of moving anything, but with the intention of keeping the lever from being moved by an opposing force. Movements take time and are properly the objects of intentions rather than volitions. Volitions do not plan ahead, not even very slightly. They do not *plan* at all; they *execute*. I have an intention as to what course of movement my body is to take over the next few moments, and in light of that intention I go through a certain course of volitional activity, of voluntary exertion, over the whole period of the movement, willing at each point, in light of my perceptions, the directed force needed at that point to keep the movement on the path prescribed by my intention. When the intention is bodily movement, willing is analogous to steering with a steering wheel rather than to steering with buttons that trigger preset patterns of movement. If there are mental "triggers" of sequences of voluntary exertion (as there may be in familiar, practiced movements), the volitional activity is not the trigger but part of what it triggers.⁹

It is true that we speak of voluntarily doing with, or to, our bodies things other than exerting force with them. For example, I can voluntarily *warm my foot* by rubbing it with my hand: Over a period, I voluntarily exert force with my arm and hand in order thereby to cause my foot to become warmer. I could voluntarily exert force with my foot in a similar indirect way by manipulating it with my arm and hand. In all such cases, my *volition* – what I mean by that term – is concerned only with the bodily parts I exert *directly,* in order thereby, indirectly, to have an effect on other parts. Volition is concerned only with direct control of exertion. The further, indirect manipulation of the body is said to be done *voluntarily* only in virtue of the fact that the direct voluntary exertion is undertaken with the intention of having that further effect.

It is conceivable that a person should voluntarily cause certain effects in his body (for example, his face to redden) not by means of what I call volition – not by direct voluntary exertion (for example, by rubbing his face with his hand) – but by means of another sort of mental activity, for example, by forming certain mental images or by directing his thoughts to certain embarrassing facts. Forming

---

9 This is the chief point that distinguishes what I mean by *volition* from what Prichard (1949) means by *willing* and what Hornsby (1980) means by *trying*. And this point, together with the earlier point that the content of volition need not be desired or intended, sharply distinguish what I mean by *volition* from what is meant by some other recent writers who have reintroduced talk of volitions into the theory of action, namely, Goldman (1976), Sellars (1976), Davis (1979, chs. 1 and 2), and Zimmerman (1984). For each of them, the content of what he calls a *willing* or a *volition* does "look ahead" (or can do so), encompassing an action or activity extended in time, like swimming a whole stroke or a whole length or uttering a sentence or signing one's name. Since what these philosophers mean does have this feature and implies intending or desiring the willed content, it is fundamentally different from what I mean by *volition*.

Davis's account differs from mine in still another way. He uses *volition* to name a functionally defined mental process that is *not* part of our experience but is posited by theory as causing the rest of the action and the agent's belief that she is acting (Davis, 1979, pp. 15–25); whereas I mean by the term something of which we are directly aware. It is noteworthy that Davis's functional definition of "volition to do an *A*" (Davis, 1979, p. 20) fits what I mean by the term (when *A* is suitably restricted to bodily exertion in the immediate present). It is possible that, were the part of our experience of voluntary exertion I mean by *volition* properly picked out for him, Davis would be inclined to identify it with what he means (or with part of what he means) rather than to deny that we experience volition.

a mental image is not a volition to blush, even if one does it with the intention of thereby causing one's face to redden. This sort of mental act is utterly different phenomenally from the mental activity that is the nonperceptual part of our experience of voluntary exertion, the mental activity I am calling volition. And, most important, even when it is intended to produce a bodily effect, it does not have the production of that effect as part of *its* intentional content. (I suspect that people who have acquired the ability voluntarily to change the rate of their heartbeat – in a direct way – do it by means of mental activity that is more like forming mental images or directing one's thoughts along certain lines than it is like volition.)

We can speak of voluntarily *ceasing* to exert force. I may voluntarily relax my arm, ending a period of exerting it. This involves no new sort of mental action, for voluntarily ceasing to exert is just ceasing the volition, ceasing to will, to exert. This is not the same, note, as ceasing voluntarily to exert, which could occur without one's *voluntarily ceasing,* that is, while one continues to will to exert (if, for example, one's motor nerves suddenly and unexpectedly become incapacitated).

Let us return to the question of what sort of proposition captures the instantaneous content of volition. Is it simply that a certain part of the body should just then exert a certain force in a certain direction? That, of course, is always part of the content, but it cannot be the whole of it. For if the bodily part just then exerted the force contemplated in the volitional content, but it did not do so *because* the subject willed it, then not everything the subject willed would have been carried out. When I exert voluntarily, I will, not just that my body exert, but that *I* exert with my body. I will, not just exerting, but my exerting, exerting caused by me. The intentional object of my volition is not just my body's exertion but my voluntary control of its exertion. I will that my willing – this very willing of whose content we speak – cause the exertion. The content refers to the volition of which it is the content and says that this volition should cause the body to exert in a certain way.

A similar thing, by the way, is true of intention. The content of an intention to act, fully spelled out, must refer to that very intention and give it a role in ensuring that the action comes about. If I intend to do a certain thing, I intend to do it intentionally: I intend that I do it and that my doing it be a carrying out of that very intention. It will be a carrying out of that intention only if I do it at least partly in order to fulfill that intention.[10] This feature, that their content gives them a role in bringing about the realization of the content, marks off intention and volition from other conative propositional attitudes such as desire, wish, and hope. I can desire something without desiring that my desire have any role in bringing it about.

Returning to volition, we can say that my volition at an instant can be ascribed to me in a proposition of the following form: I will that this willing cause my bodily part B to exert force of degree F in direction D. Here F is a certain *range* of degrees of force and D is a certain *range* of directions. What I will is, of course, never absolutely precise and determinate with respect to the degree or direction of the force. When I begin to move a lever, the degree and direction of the force exerted by my arm, as these things might be measured by precision instruments, could vary within certain limits and still fit the content of my volition. Gaining more finely tuned control of one's body is at least partly a matter of becoming able to will contents that are more determinate.

From my being able to *think* a certain determinate degree of force or direction, it does not follow that I am able to *will* it. In thought I can distinguish indefinitely many degrees of force in the range between the least and the greatest that I can voluntarily exert with my arm, but in volition I cannot distinguish so many. Suppose that I exert a force with my arm against a device that very precisely measures the force. Although it seems to me that I keep the force constant, the device shows that it varies continually up and down. When I will to exert ever so slightly more force than I had been exerting, the device shows an increment. If I were asked to increase the force I exert by just half that increment, I would understand the request but I would not be able to do it at will, to voluntarily control the exertion that finely. Similarly for the direction of the force: What I can discriminate in thought I need not be able to discriminate in volition.

How is it possible for volition to have such content as I have been talking about? As I go about my voluntary exertions, do I have in

10 Harman (1976, Section II) argues for a very similar point about intention, which he puts this way (p. 441): "The intention to do A is the intention that, because of that very intention, it is guaranteed that one will do A". Searle (1983, ch. 3) ascribes the same sort of self-reference to what he calls *intention in action*.

my mind a constantly changing representation of these details of what I will – the bodily part(s) and the degree(s) and the direction(s) of the force(s) specified to certain limits? Do I perhaps have constantly changing mental images that express or depict the contents of my volition? This seems implausible, but such a view has been put forward. William James, in his chapter on the will in *Principles of Psychology,* took such a view of the matter. He held that volitions are constituted by *kinesthetic images,* derived from previous kinesthetic perceptions, of the movements willed. It is a view like this that helps to give volition a bad name.

One is lured into such a view, I suppose, by the thought that there is no other way in which the facts about the subject can determine what the content of her willing is. But this thought is doubly wrong. First, it is wrong in supposing that a mental representation – whether image, sentence, or other – *can* by itself determine a content. No picture by itself determines what it represents; no sentence by itself determines what proposition it expresses. It is always something extrinsic to these things that determines what they represent. What a mental picture or sentence represents is determined by what its subject is disposed to do with respect to it. Second, the doubly wrong thought overlooks the possibility that, if it is such other facts that determine what a picture or sentence in the mind represents, then similar sorts of facts can determine a content for a volition (or intention or belief) without there being anything like a picture or symbol in the mind that counts as a representation of that content.

James's view is as plausible a representational account of what determines volitional content as can be found, and yet it flies in the face of our actual experience. We find in our experience of voluntary exertion very little of the kinesthetic imagery James postulates. Consider what your experience would be like if your every voluntary exertion were accompanied by a mental image of the kinesthetic perception of that exertion. (The mental image of the exertion must be distinct from the perception of it, since the perception is an effect of the exertion and the image is, on James's theory, its cause.) Such an experience would, I should think, be quite bewildering, something like a kinesthetic counterpart of double vision.

There is no need to think of volition as containing any representation of its content – by kinesthetic images, mental diagrams, mental sentences, or the like – in order to explain how volition can have the intrinsic content it does. This can be explained instead in terms of a dispositional feature of volition. Willing exertion of sort *W* entails, roughly, being disposed to be surprised by kinesthetic perception of exertion contrary to sort *W* and to be not surprised by kinesthetic perception of exertion of sort *W*. This is not quite right (for a reason I will come to shortly). It is more accurate to put it this way: Willing exertion of sort *W* entails being disposed to regard perception of that sort of exertion as perception of what one is willing (what one is "trying" to do) and to regard contrary perception in the contrary way, as perception of something incompatible with what one is trying to do.

This way of defining the content of volition does not mean that my volition has content only when I perceive my exertions. If I will to exert in a certain way with my arm but fail to perceive the resulting exertion (because, say, my kinesthetic perception fails to function), there may still be present what makes it true that the exertion fits the content of my volition, namely, its being the case that if I *had* accurately perceived that exertion (within the limits of my perceptual capacity), then I *would* have regarded it as the exertion I was trying to make.

The fact that volitional content is determined in this way does mean, however, that the fine tuning of volitional content is limited by the subject's capacity to discriminate in kinesthetic perception parts of the body and degrees and directions of force that they exert. If I am unable, in my kinesthetic perception, to discriminate between two very slightly different degrees of force that my arm might exert, then I am unable to be disposed to regard my perceiving the one as perceiving what I am willing and to regard my perceiving the other as perceiving something contrary to what I am willing; for my perception of both would be just the same. (Hence, improvement in the precision of the exertions one can execute at will requires improvement in the discrimination of one's kinesthetic perception.) James had the view that what one can will at any given time is limited to what one has kinesthetically perceived at some prior time. His reason was that what one can kinesthetically *image* is limited to what one has already perceived. My view is that what one can will is limited to what one is currently *able* to *perceive* kinesthetically. My reason is that this limits what one can be surprised at should it fail to occur.

So far, I have been saying what volition is. Now let us consider what *voluntary exertion of the body* is. Wherever there is voluntary exertion, there must be volition. How are the two related? Does volition cause voluntary exertion? No. Voluntary exertion *begins* with, not results from, volition. Volition is the initial *part,* not the cause, of voluntary exertion. It is, of course, only a part and not the whole. What must be added to get the whole? More precisely, in order to have the fact that

> I voluntarily exerted force (of degree) F (in direction) D with (bodily part) B

what must be added to the fact that

> I willed to exert force FD with B?

One correct answer to this question is fairly obvious. We must add that B's exerting FD did occur and that it was caused in the right sort of way by the volition. If there was just my willing to exert force forward with my arm, and my arm's exerting force forward and *no* causal connection between them, then obviously there would not be *my voluntarily exerting* force with my arm. Suppose, for example, that, unknown to me, my arm was caused to exert the force by a stimulation of the appropriate motor nerves through wires attached to them that were controlled by other people, and suppose that this happened coincidentally just as I willed to exert my arm. Then I would have had a nice *illusion* of voluntarily exerting my arm.

Clearly, a causal connection between the willing and the body's exertion is required. But not just any sort of causal connection will do. The volition must cause the body's exertion via the right sort of mechanism. If my willing to exert force FD with my arm does cause my arm to exert force $FD,$ it does not follow from this alone that I voluntarily exert force FD with my arm. For it may have been too fortuitous that the content of my volition was matched by the exertion that the volition caused. The circumstances on which depended the volition's having that result in my body may have failed to be such that, had the volition been different in content, the bodily result would have been correspondingly different. There may not have been involved any standing mechanism via which the volition had its bodily result and which would have translated any other volition I might instead have engaged in into a content-matching bodily effect. The volition causes the exertion in the way necessary to make the whole structure voluntary exertion only if it does so via a standing mechanism that is sufficiently *match-ensuring*.

We have plenty of evidence that the normal mechanism that reliably translates volition into a matching bodily result lies in the brain and the efferent neural system stemming from the brain. We can imagine cases in which the volition-translating mechanism fails to be sufficiently match-ensuring by imagining that this normal mechanism is tampered with. Imagine, for example, an artificial device installed in (or on) a person's body that takes the efferent output of the person's brain as its input and, as a consequence of this input, produces stimulation of the motor nerves to the person's muscles. Imagine this device set so that no matter what the input – that is, no matter what the content of the person's volition – the output is the same: Whether the person wills to exert the arm or leg or vocalizing mechanism or anything else, the result is always, say, a contraction of the muscles that bend the right index finger. Or imagine that the device is set so that it produces a different output for every different input, but only in a very few cases, and in a nonsystematic way, does the output match the content of the volition that produces the input. In imagining such cases, we are imagining people who have been deprived of voluntary control of their bodies. Nothing that such a person's body does can be considered a voluntary exertion of that person, even if occasionally what it does happens to match the content of a volition of hers that causes it.

This is not because of the *artificiality* of the device inserted into the person's neural system. If the artificial device did as good a job of translating volitions into content-matching bodily results as the natural system does, then the person who had the artificial device would not be deprived of voluntary control of her body. She would merely have an artificial component in her nervous system. That system would be functionally equivalent to the natural system, and there would be no reason to deny that it enables her to exercise voluntary control of her body. The other people we imagined lack voluntary control simply because their artificial devices are not sufficiently like the natural system with respect to the matching between volitional input and exertional output that they stand ready to produce.

We now have all the components we need to formulate a nontrivial, sufficient condition for the truth of propositions of the form

I voluntarily exerted *FD* with *B*.

Such a proposition will be true if

(1) *B* exerted *FD* and
(2) this was caused by my willing to exert *FD* with *B* via a standing mechanism that is sufficiently match-ensuring.

This sufficient condition fails, however, to be *necessary*. There are two different reasons. One has to do with the fact that any bodily part contains indefinitely many smaller parts. If some bodily part $B^\star$ exerts a certain force $F^\star$ in a certain direction $D^\star$, then, if *B* is a part of $B^\star$, it follows that *B* exerts a certain force *F* in a certain direction *D*. And if I voluntarily exerted $F^\star D^\star$ with $B^\star$, then it follows that I voluntarily exerted *FD* with *B*. (For example, when I exert a strong force forward with my right hand, I ipso facto exert a strong force forward with the pisiform carpal bone in my right hand.) But it does not follow that I *willed* to exert *FD* with *B*. For besides the possibility that I may be utterly ignorant of the existence of such a part of my body (how many of us know all the bones and ligaments making up the hand?), the content of my volition can be concerned only with bodily parts I can discriminate in kinesthetic perception, and these do not include all the parts of the parts I can so discriminate. We allow for this sort of way in which the description of the voluntary exertion can differ from the volitional content if we replace the sufficient condition given above with the following weaker one:

(1) *B* exerted *FD,* and
there are $B^\star$, $F^\star$, and $D^\star$ such that
(2) $B^\star$ exerted $F^\star D^\star$,
(3) (2) entails (1),
(4) I willed to exert $F^\star D^\star$ with $B^\star$, and
(5) (2) was caused by (4) via a sufficiently match-ensuring mechanism.

The other reason our first sufficient condition was stronger than necessary has to do with the fact that in the volitional content, the degree and direction parameters of the force vector are never absolutely precise but always to some extent indeterminate. Any degree of force falling within a certain range of degrees or any direction falling within a certain range of directions will fit the volitional content. This means that if I voluntarily exerted force $F'D'$ with *B*, and "*F*" and "*D*" are more precise specifications of the force I exerted, then it follows that I voluntarily exerted force *FD* with *B*.

And this is so even though the content of my volition was not so precise.

This consideration reveals that our latest sufficient condition is still too strong to be necessary. For instance, it may be true that I voluntarily exerted FD with B, even though FD is more determinate than anything entailed for B by (2) or by any other accurate specification of my volitional content. We need to allow for the following four ways in which (1) – the description of the voluntary exertion engaged in, B *exerted FD* – may relate to the volitional content:

(a) (1) is or is entailed by the volitional content.
(b) B is not the bodily part contemplated in the volitional content, but rather some part thereof, but FD is the force vector for B entailed by the volitional content.
(c) Although B is the bodily part contemplated in the volitional content, FD is more determinate than what is contemplated in the volitional content.
(d) B is not the bodily part contemplated in the volitional content but is some part thereof, nor is FD the force vector for B entailed by the volitional content but is more determinate than it.

Our first sufficient condition accommodates only (a), and our second one accommodates only (a) and (b). We can accommodate (c) and (d) as well by simply replacing part (3) of our second condition, the part that requires (2) to entail (1). Instead of requiring B^* *exerted* F^*D^* to entail B *exerted FD*, let us require it to entail B *exerted F'D'* where $F'D'$ is entailed by but possibly less determinate than FD. Thus the entire condition will be as follows:

(1) B exerted FD,
there are B^*, F^*, and D^* such that
(2) B^* exerted F^*D^*,
(3) there are F' and D' such that FD entails $F'D'$ and (2) entails B *exerted F'D'*,
(4) I willed to exert F^*D^* with B^*, and
(5) (2) was caused by (4) via a sufficiently match-ensuring mechanism.

I hazard the claim that this condition is both necessary and sufficient for the truth of the proposition that I voluntarily exerted FD with B.

THE POSSIBILITY OF MISMATCH
BETWEEN CONTENT AND EFFECT

It is possible, I have supposed, that volition should cause bodily exertion that fails to match the volition's content. The mismatch could be systematic and drastic. There could, for example, be a device that would take all volitional input concerned with exertion of the *left* leg and produce output that causes exertion of the *right* leg. I might wake up one day to find that my legs and volitions had been "cross-wired" in this way. When I try to exert a certain force with my left leg, it is my right leg that responds, and vice versa. After I discover this, I no longer expect the exertions resulting from my leg volitions to match the volitions' content. (This is why I said earlier that it is not quite right to define the volitional content in terms of what would or would not *surprise* me.) Then I can intentionally cause the right leg to exert a certain force by trying to exert it with the left leg. (Notice that to do so would *not* be voluntarily to exert that force with the right leg, according to the claim I made at the end of the preceding section. This seems acceptable, since we can say that it would nonetheless be *intentionally* to exert it.)

But how contingent can this connection be? Is it conceivable, for instance, that day after day, month after month, year after year, in a long career of volitional activity concerned with my legs, all of this volition should continue to be cross-wired? Could there be a person who is always this way, from infancy on, who learns early, or perhaps knows innately, that in order to cause exertion of one leg, she must will exertion of the other?

I think that these extremes are bare conceptual possibilities but that, in the very nature of what determines volitional content, there is a reason why they are extremely unlikely to occur. The content of one's volition at any given time is determined by what one is at that time disposed to recognize as kinesthetic perception of what one is willing. As the cross-wiring case illustrates, there is no conceptual necessity that this should coincide with the kinesthetic perception that one then *intends* one's volition to produce. On the other hand, if a systematic disparity between volitional contents and resulting exertions should be "wired in" so as to persist for a while, and if the subject, by knowing of the disparity, is able eventually to bring her *intentions* into line with the exertions she volitionally produces, then there is no conceptual necessity that over a long enough time the volitional contents should not be able to adjust to the contents of the intentions, without any changing of the connections between motor neurons and the volitional center(s) of the brain. In the nature of what determines volitional content, there is no conceptual bar to supposing that the circumstance of its being continually and systematically in conflict with accompanying intention should eventually cause the volitional content, what it seems to one that one is willing, to change so as to coincide with the content of the accompanying intention. The dissonant and inefficient experience of its seeming to one that one tries to exert the left leg in order to exert the right leg eventually gives way, simply by sufficient repetition and without any decision to change either the volition or the intention, to the more harmonious and tolerable experience of its seeming to one that one wills to exert the *right* leg in order to exert the right leg.

In visual perception, there is a well-known phenomenon that is analogous to what I am imagining here. A person can have visual impressions about the vertical or horizontal orientation of objects she sees that conflict systematically with her other sorts of perception of the same objects: The world *looks* upside down, but kinesthetic–tactual exploration reveals it to be right side up. Such a conflict of perceptions is cognitively very inefficient and hard to tolerate over the long run. It is not likely to be the mode of operation for sense perception that nature would make the innate norm. And we find that, when it is artificially produced by inverting spectacles, the subject's visual impressions tend over sufficient time to adjust their content to coincide with that of the subject's perception in the other modes.

Volitional content is, in a way, anticipation of kinesthetic perception, but it is anticipation that could conflict both with the perception actually produced by the volition and with the subject's *intention* regarding the perception to be produced by the volition. Such conflict would be very difficult to live with. It is not likely to be the mode of volitional control of our bodies that nature would endow us with. And if it were produced artificially by cross-wiring, the ensuing conflict of what is volitionally "anticipated" with what is intended would, nature permitting, be likely to resolve itself in the long run in favor of the content of intention. After enough willing to exert my left leg in order to exert my right leg and being successful in this maneuver, it is likely that willing to exert my left leg would come to *seem like* willing to exert my right leg, which is to say that it would come to *be* willing to exert my right leg. Some such adjustment would, at any rate, be necessary for my again becoming efficient at operating those limbs. Systematic mismatching of volitional contents to volitional effects should be inherently unstable.

3

The individuation of actions

Our definition of an action in Chapter 1 tells us how to select from among canonical personal-event-designators those that designate actions. But to know what makes an action-designator is not yet to have a complete understanding of what makes an action. For canonical action-designators are not correlated one to one with actions. Distinct designators do not always designate distinct actions. For example, it is natural to think that although «*S*'s willing to exert force with her hand at *t*» and «*S*'s raising her hand at *t*» designate distinct actions, «*S*'s raising her hand at *t*» and «*S*'s slowly raising her right hand at *t*» designate the same action (given that each of these designators is canonical and thus uniquely picks out a single action). But our criterion for picking out action-designators does not tell us what guides such a judgment. This chapter takes up the task of developing a criterion for deciding when distinct (canonical) action-designators designate distinct actions.

We need to be concerned here only with designators in which the type of the action designated is made fully explicit. Consider a designator of the form «*S*'s doing this morning the same thing she did yesterday that *R* complained about», one that uniquely picks out a particular action. It picks it out as being of a certain type (the type *S* did yesterday that *R* complained about), but it does not, just in virtue of its content, tell us what that type is. That is to say, someone who fully understands the content of this designator, and knows that it does pick out a particular action as being of a particular type, could still fail to know what that type is. The same would be true of a designator that gives some information, but not complete information, as to the type of the action that it picks out, such as "*S*'s making a movement with her arm just now of the same sort that caused her such pain a few minutes ago". This tells us that *S*'s action was a particular sort of moving of her arm, but it does not tell us what sort. These designators fail to make fully explicit the type of the action designated, because the designator picks out the type through some external property it has (such as having a token that caused S pain).[1] More generally, a designator fails to make fully explicit the type of the action it picks out just in case one could fully understand the designator and that it implies that the action is of a particular sort without knowing what that sort is – that is, there is some other specification of the sort such that, though one fully understands it as well, one could fail to know that it picks out that same sort.

The question as to whether or not two given designators designate the same action can be conveniently addressed only when those designators do make fully explicit the type of action each picks out. This is because the answer to that question depends very much on the type that each designator implies that the action it designates belongs to. So let us add to the features of a *canonical* action-designator the requirement that the designator be fully explicit as to the type of action specified.

Several competing views on this question of action individuation have been put forward, but there is one important point about it that is not controversial. Those pairs of canonical action-designators about which it may reasonably be disputed whether they designate the same action all have to each other a certain relation that we may call *belonging to the same action tree*.[2] This relation can be defined in terms of the GEN relation, which we used in Chapter 1 in the inductive clause of our definition of when a personal-event-designator is an action-designator. The GEN relation was defined as follows: Given that «S's U-ing at $t^\star$» and «S's V-ing at t» are canonical action-designators, the action designated by the first has the GEN relation to that designated by the second just in case (1) «S's V-ing at t» BY «S's U-ing at $t^\star$», (2) «S's V-ing at t» is of the form «S's X-ing at t by U-ing at $t^\star$», or (3) «S's V-ing at t» is of the form «S's U-ing at $t^\star$ in circumstance C»and is such that some action-designator has the BY relation to «S's U-ing at $t^\star$» because it has the BY relation to it.

---

1 Goldman (1970) appears to make the same distinction when he says (pp. 12–13), "although we can *refer* to this property [of being blue] with the expression 'the color property of the sky', this phrase does not *express* this property in the way that 'being blue' *expresses* it".
2 This idea is derived from that of an *act-tree* in Goldman (1970, ch. 2).

The notion of the same action tree is defined as follows:

> Two canonical action-designators belong to the same action tree just in case they refer to the same agent and one has the ancestral of the GEN relation to the other, or there is a third canonical action-designator that belongs to the same action tree as each of them.

So, for example, all the action-designators given in the following list A would belong to the same action tree, and so also would all those given in list B, if their BY or GEN relations were as shown.

A. 1. «S's moving her hand at t_1»
   2. «S's flipping the light switch at t_2»
   3. «S's turning on the light at t_3»
   4. «S's waking her husband at t_4»
   5. «S's waking the only man in the room at t_4»
   6. «S's flipping the switch by moving her hand at t_2»
   2 BY 1, 3 BY 2, 4 BY 3, 5 BY 3, 1 GEN 6
B. 1. «S's willing (volition) to exert force upward with her arm and hand at t_1»
   2. «S's voluntarily exerting force upward with her arm and hand at t_1»
   3. «S's raising her hand at t_1»
   4. «S's raising her right hand at t_1»
   5. «S's slowly raising her hand at t_1»
   6. «S's raising her hand just after she has heard the chair of the meeting say "And those opposed?" at t_1»
   7. «S's voting against a proposal at t_2»
   8. «S's offending R at t_3»
   2 BY 1, 3 BY 2, 4 BY 2, 5 BY 2, 3 GEN 6, 7 BY 6, 8 BY 7
   (because the proposal S voted against was originated by R)

The various contrary positions on the question of how actions should be individuated can be divided into three groups.

1. At the minimizing extreme (individuating actions most coarsely), we have the view that any two designators on the same action tree designate the same action.[3] This view has the consequence that, for example, designators A.1 and A.2 designate the very same action (given that A.2 has the BY relation to A.1). This seems counterintuitive. The concrete chunk of the past designated by (A.2) «S's flipping the light switch at t_2», includes something more than is included in the chunk designated by (A.1) «S's moving her hand at t_1», namely, something that happened to the light switch as a result of S's moving her hand.
2. At the maximizing extreme (individuating actions most finely), we have Alvin Goldman's view that two designators designate distinct actions if

---

3 This view has been put forward by Anscombe (1958), Davidson (1963, 1967, 1971), D'Arcy (1963), Shwayder (1965), and Hornsby (1980).

they ascribe to the agent distinct action properties.[4] This view has the consequence that, for example, designators B.3 and B.5 designate distinct actions, for the property of raising one's hand is distinct from the property of slowly raising one's hand. But this seems counterintuitive. (B.5) «S's slowly raising her hand at t_1» seems to pick out the same chunk of the past as does (B.3) «S's raising her hand at t_1» (given that at t there was just one raising of a hand by S); it just gives a bit more information about its intrinsic nature.

3. Between these extremes (where I am inclined to be), it is possible to take various different positions that say that some designators belonging to the same action tree designate the same action and others don't.[5]

The disagreement between Goldman's extreme maximizing position and all the others involves also a disagreement as to what metaphysical category of thing action-designators designate, what category of thing actions are. Goldman takes an action to be *an exemplifying of an action property* (he also calls an action property an action *type,* and he speaks of an exemplifying of such a type as an *act-token*). An exemplifying of an action property occurs just in case there is an individual (or individuals if the property is polyadic) and a time such that that individual exemplifies (or those individuals exemplify) that property at that time. Goldman (following Kim[6]) gives the following criterion of individuation for this sort of entity: One exemplifying of a property is identical to another just in case the individual (or the ordered n-tuple of individuals), the property, and the time involved in the one are identical, respectively, to those involved in the other.[7]

If this is the sort of thing that an exemplifying of a property is and Goldman is right that actions are exemplifyings of properties, then he is right about the individuation of action: Nonequivalent action-designators do represent distinct exemplifyings of properties, given that two predicates signify the same property only if they are necessarily equivalent. In order to disagree with Goldman on the individuation question, the extreme minimizers and those of us in one or another middle position must claim that actions are not

4 Goldman (1970, p. 10).
5 Thomson (1977), for example, takes such a position.
6 Kim (1966, p. 231).
7 Goldman (1970, p. 10). This criterion would seem to need refining, in view of the possibility of simultaneous double exemplifying of the same property by the same individual, but the refinements should not affect what I want to say about it. Goldman makes a suggestion regarding such a refinement at p. 11, note 13, which is to add a fourth component to action tokens.

this rather abstract sort of particular that Goldman says they are but something more concrete. But we must explain what this more concrete sort of thing is. In particular, we must give a criterion of individuation for it. I will propose one in due course.

The sort of thing we various nonmaximizers want to make actions out to be need not be affected by *our* differences on the individuation question. The disagreement between the extreme minimizing position and the various middle positions on that question is a disagreement about how certain action-designators work to pick out particular things, not necessarily about what ontological category the things they pick out belong to.

The extreme minimizers suppose that the action designated by all the designators on the same action tree is always just the basic action that is at the root of the tree. It is the minimal thing the agent had to do, in the circumstances, in order to perform the action designated. In their view, that is all the agent really does: "the rest is up to nature", as Davidson puts it.[8] They think of a nonbasic-action-designator as identifying externally, in terms of its consequences or its circumstances, the very same action picked out by a certain basic action-designator. (Their view as to what is a basic action-designator may differ from mine, that it designates a simple mental act, but the general idea we can all agree on is that «S's V-ing at t» is basic just in case it does not designate an aggregate of actions and no other action-designator has to it the GEN relation.) So they would regard, for example, (A.2) «S's flipping the light switch at t_2» as picking out the basic action by which S flipped the light switch (on my view, this would be a certain chunk of volitional activity on S's part, but on Davidson's view, for example, it would be S's voluntarily moving her body in a certain way); it picks it out in terms of its result, as the basic action that caused the switch to be flipped.

I, on the other hand, like others in middle positions, view that sort of designator as describing the action it picks out in terms of its further *components* beyond the basic action. I find it natural to think of what is denoted by, for example, (B.3) «S's raising her hand at t_1» as including among its parts not only the volition denoted by B.1, but also the result of that volition implied by B.3, namely, S's hand's rising; or, for another example, to think of what is designated by (B.8) «S's offending R at t_3» as including among its parts not only

---

8 Davidson (1980, p. 59).

the action designated by (B.7) «S's voting against a proposal at t_2», but also the result of that action implied by B.8, namely, R's being offended by S's action. I also find it natural (and here some middlers might part company with me) to think of the action designated by, for example, (B.6) «S's raising her hand just after she has heard the chair of the meeting say "And those opposed?" at t_1» as including among its parts not only the action designated by B.3, but also the *circumstance* of that action implied by B.6, namely, the chair's having said what he did just before that action. The action designated by (B.7) «S's voting against a proposal at t_2» adds another layer of circumstance to that designated by B.6, namely, the existence then and there of a convention according to which, if S raises her hand just after the chair has said "And those opposed?", then she thereby votes against the proposal before the meeting. Such a circumstance may be fairly extensive in a particular concrete realization, for it comprises all the particular events and states in virtue of which it is true that there existed then and there that convention. To take a different sort of example, «S's jumping further this morning than she ever has before» designates an action that includes not only a particular jumping of S's this morning, but the circumstance that prior to it S had not jumped as far as she did in that jump. This circumstance includes all of S's previous jumps, for it is their all being shorter than S's jump this morning.

In these examples and many others that could be given, an action and a result or circumstance of it together form a significant whole that the agent made to exist by that action, such a whole as the agent could have intended to make exist (though she need not have so intended). This *whole* can be thought of as something that this person qua agent contributed to the world: Its parts that are not actions of the agent were either caused by him or else were already in place, so that his action completed the whole. Therefore this whole can be thought of as itself an *action* of that agent, despite the fact that not all of its parts are actions of his. An action plus a result or a circumstance of it make a larger action that has the smaller action as its core. Thus an action may be built up in several layers, each new layer being some result or circumstance of the core action to which it is added.

Actions are events that have a layered structure. At the ultimate base or core lies mental action of the agent, typically volition. The parts added to the core to make a larger action (for example, the resulting exertion of force by the agent's body or the circumstance of the agent's intending by that volition so to exert her body) and the parts added to those larger actions to make still larger ones (for example, the opening of a window resulting from the body's exertion of force or the circumstance of there being an understanding that the window's opening would be a signal that the agent wanted help) are typically not actions of that agent (though an action *can* have another action of the same agent as an outer layer, either a consequence or a circumstance of the core action, for example, S's breaking a promise by voting against the motion after having promised to vote for it or S's causing herself to telephone R by posting a reminder to do so). That actions have such a layered structure means that distinct actions can have the same parts. For instance, S's action of pressing a button because R told her to do so is distinct from R's action of getting S to press a button by telling her to do so. The two actions have the same parts: an action of S's, an action of R's, and a causal relation between them. But one is an action of S's, having volition of S as its ultimate core and R's action as an outer layer of circumstance, and the other is an action of R's having volition of R as its ultimate core and S's action as an outer layer of consequence.[9]

On this way of looking at actions, the designators (B.3) «S's raising her hand at t_1», (B.4) «S's raising her right hand at t_1», and (B.5) «S's slowly raising her hand at t_1» still all designate the same action, for the core volition is the same in what they designate and none adds any *result* or *circumstance* to what is designated by one of the others. In the action designated by (B.4) «S's raising her *right* hand at t_1», there is nothing that was caused by or a circumstance of the action designated by (B.3) «S's raising her hand at t_1»; similarly for the action designated by B.5. B.4 and B.5 just give us *more specific* descriptions of the internal features of the same concrete whole that B.3 describes. On the other hand, (B.2) «S's voluntarily exerting force upward with her arm and hand at t_1» obviously adds a result to the basic action designated by (B.1) «S's willing (volition) to exert force upward with her arm and hand at t_1». What about B.3 vis-à-

---

9 Complex events that are not actions can be structured in a similar way. The event of the tree's causing the power line to break by falling on it and the power line's breaking as a result of the tree's falling on it are distinct events, though they have the same parts. The core of one event is the change in the tree, and the core of the other is the change in the power line.

vis B.2? B.3 adds a result to B.2, namely, the hand's rising. For if the circumstances had been different, the same exertion of force in an upward direction with the arm and hand would have occurred without that result occurring – if, for example, some opposing force had prevented the motion.

The designators (A.4) «S's waking her husband at t_4» and (A.5) «S's waking the only man in the room at t_4» show a need for further refinement of our account. Given that S's husband was the only man in the room, these two *could* be used to designate the same action, despite the fact that A.5 implies a circumstance not implied by A.4, namely, that the waking occurred in a room, and the fact that A.4 implies a circumstance not implied by A.5, namely, that the man S wakened was married to S. Whether these implications do add parts to the actions designated in these cases depends on the users' intent in employing the descriptive singular terms that the designators contain. When we come (later in this chapter) to give a criterion for the case where two action-designators designate the same action, we can circumvent the complications created by this relativity to the user's intent if we give our criterion for canonical designators only and if we stipulate about canonical designators that the circumstances and consequences that are part of the actions they designate are exactly those implied by their descriptive contents. Thus, if the user of (A.4) «S's waking her husband at t_4» did not intend to include in the action designated the circumstance that the person S wakened was married to S (the user did not think of that circumstance as part of the significant whole S contributed to the world to which the user wished to direct attention, but mentioned the marital relation only in order to help the hearer identify the wakened person), then the designator she has used is not canonical for the action she intended to designate; a canonical designator for that action would perhaps be «S's waking N at t_4», where N is a singular term lacking the descriptive content of "her husband" but referring to the person S waked, perhaps a proper name or a demonstrative like "that person".

THREE ARGUMENTS AGAINST MINIMIZING

I now postpone further explanation of my own view about individuation in order to examine three arguments in support of the view that at least some designators belonging to the same action tree designate distinct actions. They are the argument from BY relations, the argument from causal–explanatory relations, and the argument from temporal relations.[10] The argument from causal–explanatory relations is the only one of the three that supports Goldman's most extreme and counterintuitive nonidentity claims. Most of the nonidentity claims supported by the argument from BY relations and all of them supported by the argument from temporal relations are ones that I, and probably most other middlers, would wish to make; thus those two are really arguments against the minimizing extreme rather than arguments for the maximizing extreme. It seems to me that only the argument from temporal relations holds up on examination.

The argument from BY relations

This argument[11] is intended to show the nonidentity of any two actions such that the designator of one has the BY relation to the designator of the other. The argument deduces its conclusion from two premises:

I. The BY relation is antisymmetrical. That is, given any two action-designators X and Y, if «X BY Y» is true, then «Y BY X»is false.
II. The BY relation is extensional in the following sense: For any action-designators, X, Y, and Z, if X BY Y, then X BY Z if Y and Z designate the same action, and Z BY Y if X and Z designate the same action.

Given these premises, one can easily show by *reductio ad absurdum* that, for any action-designators X and Y, not both «X and Y designate the same action» and «X BY Y» are true. Simply assume the contradictory of this conclusion and use (I) and (II) to deduce a contradiction:

1. X and Y designate the same action.
2. X BY Y.
3. Y BY Y.   from 1 and 2 by II
4. Y BY X.   from 1 and 3 by II
5. Not (Y BY X).   from 2 by I

As far as I can see, premise I is true: The BY relation is antisymmetrical. But there is reason to doubt premise II, that the BY

10 The first two of these originated, as far as I know, in Goldman (1970). The argument from temporal relations was put forward in Davis (1970) and Thomson (1971a) and endorsed in Goldman (1971).
11 See Goldman (1970, pp. 4–5). I here put the argument in my own way.

relation is extensional. Suspicion about this premise arises when one notices that this same sort of argument can be given to support claims of nonidentity that seem clearly to be false.[12] For example, let X and Y be, respectively, «S's playing a C-major chord at t» and «S's simultaneously playing a C, an E, and a G at t». Then 1 and 2 in the preceding argument form seem both to be true: S played a C chord by simultaneously playing a C, an E, and a G; but S's playing a C chord *was* S's simultaneously playing those three notes. Or let X be «S's typing "by" at t» and let Y be «S's first typing b and then typing y at t»; again, both «X BY Y» and «X and Y designate the same action» seem to be true. These examples do not counter premise I: For both pairs of substitutions, «Y BY X» is false. It would not be true to say that S simultaneously played a C, an E, and a G *by* playing a C chord, or that S first typed b and then y by typing *by*. So these examples must counter premise II.

These examples illustrate a general recipe for constructing examples where both «X and Y designate the same action» and «X BY Y» are true. Make Y designate the same action as X, but give a fuller analysis of the subactions that this action *consisted in*. As an abbreviated way of expressing this relation between X and Y, let us say that X CONSISTED IN Y. It is clear that the CONSISTED IN relation is antisymmetrical; and so, since it entails that the relata designate the same action, it is clear that it is nonextensional because, as the preceding argument shows, no relation that obtains between identical items can be both antisymmetrical and extensional. Since, as the examples given illustrate, both identity and the BY relation are entailed by the CONSISTS IN relation, the BY relation cannot be extensional. Thus premise II of the argument from BY relations is false.

The argument from causal–explanatory relations

It is by this argument[13] that Goldman supports the claims of non-identity that, to many of us, seem the most counterintuitive. Consider, for example, designators (B.3) «S's raising her hand at t_1» and (B.5) «S's slowly raising her hand at t_1». Prima facie, it seems per-

---

12 It would surprise me if Goldman would not feel obliged to agree, despite the fact that these nonidentity claims follow from his criterion of identity.

13 See Goldman (1970, pp. 2–4). Again I put the argument in my own way.

verse to hold that they designate different actions. It seems evident that they designate one and the same action and that B.5 just gives more information about the manner of performance of that action than does B.3.

But Goldman has an argument against this intuition, based on the ground that something enters into the causal explanation of the action designated by B.5 that does not enter into any causal explanation of the one designated by B.3, namely, S's being reluctant to offend R. That is, it is true that S raised her hand slowly because she was reluctant to offend R but *not* true that she raised her hand because she was reluctant to offend R. And, Goldman says, "if A and A' are one and the same action, . . . one would expect them, if they are caused at all, to be caused by the same set of events or states of affairs."[14] And the action designated by B.5 may causally explain something that the one designated by B.3 does not, for example, R's feeling some comfort. Suppose that S's raising her hand slowly (in voting against R's proposal) gave R some comfort. That does not make it the case that S's raising her hand gave R some comfort. As Goldman might have said, if A and A' are one and the same action, one would expect them, if they cause anything at all, to cause the same set of events or states of affairs.

One might try to counter this argument by denying Goldman's assumptions. One might claim that the relation of causation is *not* an extensional relation, but holds between two events *only under certain descriptions* of them and not under others. Just as «Oedipus wanted to marry x» may be true under certain descriptions of x ("Jocasta", "the Queen of Thebes") and not true under others ("his mother"), so also, it might be said, «S's reluctance to offend R caused x» or «x gave R some comfort» is true under certain descriptions of x (for example, B.5) and not under others (for example, B.3).

Goldman replies to this objection that it makes causation "somehow language dependent" and that this is "unattractive".[15] I think that he has a point here. What seems to matter for statements as to what caused a thing is not the *language* used to identify the thing, but rather the *properties* by which the thing is picked out. And the reason that matters may well be that *what* is being explained is something's exemplifying a property at a time.

14 Goldman (1970, p. 3). See also Goldman (1971, p. 767).
15 Goldman (1970, p. 7).

55

I think we do better to respond to Goldman's argument by denying that the relata of causal explanations are always events or actions. We should deny, at any rate, that they are always the sort of *concrete* events or actions that we have in mind when we have the strong intuition that designators like B.3 and B.5 designate the same action. We can concede that sometimes the explanans or explananda of causal explanations are exemplifyings of properties by individuals at times, but still maintain that the events and actions of which we speak are often *not* that rather abstract sort of particular.

Goldman (1971) does offer an argument for his view that we should think of actions as exemplifyings of act properties by agents:

> since an act . . . is standardly designated by a nominalized form of an action sentence and since an action sentence associated with such a nominalization asserts that a person exemplifies a certain act property, it is natural to view the designatum of such a nominalization as an exemplifying of an act property by a person.[16]

The argument here seems to come to the following:

> «S's V-ing at t» denotes something (action or event) if and only if S exemplifies at t the property of V-ing.
> Therefore, «S's V-ing at t» denotes S's exemplifying at t the property of V-ing.

This is uncompelling. It is no better than the following argument:

> "The inventor of bifocals" denotes something if and only if some individual exemplified the property of inventing bifocals.
> Therefore, "the inventor of bifocals" denotes an individual's exemplifying the property of inventing bifocals.

Here the premise is clearly true and the conclusion clearly false: "the inventor of bifocals" denotes the *individual,* Benjamin Franklin, not any exemplifying by him of a property.

When I say "His opening the window just now was something to see", I refer with the nominalized sentence to something more concrete or determinate than merely his exemplifying just now the property of opening the window. It is not *that* which I am saying was remarkable, but rather something like the whole particular, determinate way in which he in this instance exemplified that property. But this is quite compatible with its being the case that when I say "His opening the window clumsily just now is explained by his being a bit tipsy", I *do* refer merely to his just now exemplify-

16 Goldman (1971, pp. 770–1).

ing the property of clumsily opening the window; this is shown, let us concede, by Goldman's argument, for it would not be right to say, "His opening the window just now [omitting "clumsily"] is explained by his being a bit tipsy".

We can even allow that exemplifyings of properties by individuals at times are a special sort of event, a sort that is different from the more concrete and determinate sort we often speak of. It is this special, less concrete sort of event that we refer to when we denote the explananda of certain causal explanations. And we can concede, of course, that all of Goldman's nonidentity claims with respect to this special sort of event are correct. If every designator on our B action tree (in the section "Action Trees and the Competing Views") were replaced by the corresponding designator of the form «S's exemplifying at t the property of V-ing», then, it is clear, no two of them would designate the same thing, for no two of them mention the same property. We might call exemplifyings of properties – the sort of thing Goldman says events and actions are – *abstract* events, and call the more determinate sort of thing we often refer to *concrete* events.

Other sorts of statements than ones attributing causal relations may refer to abstract events. Someone might say, for example, "I did not disapprove of her raising her hand, but I did disapprove of her raising it *slowly*". Here the speaker is referring to distinct abstract events. The speaker could, however, have conveyed the same message by referring to a single concrete event, saying, "I disapproved of that raising her hand she did then, but only for (only with respect to) its being as slow as it was".

Incidentally, one context in which we refer to actions but do not seem to be referring to Goldman's abstract actions (exemplifyings of action properties) occurs when we speak of one action's being done *by* doing another. «S's offending R by voting against R's proposal» and «S's ringing the bell by pushing the button» seem to be cases where we are *not* referring to exemplifyings of act properties. This can be seen by replacing the relevant designators with ones that do explicitly refer to exemplifyings of properties: «S's exemplifying the property of ringing the bell by exemplifying the property of pushing the button» seems wrong. It is true that the bell's exemplifying the property of ringing when it did is causally explained by S's exemplifying the property of pushing the button when she did, but that fact does *not* make it the case that S exemplified the property of ringing the bell by exemplifying the property of pushing the button. In the context «x exemplifies property F by exemplifying property G», the preposition by seems to express, not a causal relation, but instead a relation of composition or supervenience. Thus it is right to say, for example, that S exemplified the property of typing by by exemplifying the property of first typing b and then typing y immediately to the right, only because exemplifying the second property is, not a *cause* but a *manner* of exemplifying the first.

The argument from temporal relations

This argument[17] is intended to show the nonidentity of, for example, the action designated by (B.7) «S's voting against a proposal at t_2» and the action designated by (B.8) «S's offending R at t_3» by appealing to the alleged fact that the second action was not complete until R felt offended, an event that, because R was not a witness to S's voting against her proposal, occurred some time later. (t_2 and t_3 could be the same time, provided that they included both S's voting against the proposal and R's becoming offended, or it could be that part of t_3 coincides with and part is later than t_2). The argument goes as follows:

1. S's voting against a proposal at t_2 occurred some time before R became offended because of S's vote.
2. It is not the case that S's offending R at t_3 occurred some time before R became offended because of S's vote.
3. Therefore, S's voting against a proposal at t_2 was not identical to S's offending R at t_3.

A similar argument could be given for any pair of action-designators where one designator brings in a later consequence of the action designated by the other designator in the way in which B.8 brings in a consequence of the action designated by B.7 – such pairs, for example, as "S's shooting R this morning" and "S's killing R today", "S's lighting the fuse this morning" and "S's exploding the bomb this morning", or "S's putting a check in the mail last Monday" and "S's paying her utility bill last week".

What can be said against the argument from temporal relations?

---

17 See Davis (1970); Goldman (1971, pp. 767–8); Thomson (1971a); Davis (1979, pp. 29–30).

It is valid, given that the relation expressed by "occurred some time before" is extensional, which it obviously is. Premise 1 is given by hypothesis. So if there is anything wrong, it is with premise 2. This premise looks hard to deny, but the following argument might be offered against it (for convenience, the temporal index is omitted from all the action-designators):

4. S's offending R = S's causing R to become offended.
5. S's causing R to become offended = S's doing something that caused R to become offended.
6. S's doing something that caused R to become offended = S's action that caused R to become offended.
7. S's action that caused R to become offended = S's voting against a proposal.
8. Therefore, S's offending R = S's voting against a proposal.
9. Therefore, given premise 1, S's offending R did occur some time before S became offended because of R's vote.

This argument is obviously valid. And three of the four premises are undeniable: 7 is given by hypothesis, and in 4 and 6 the designator to the right of the identity sign is simply a paraphrase of the one to the left. But there seems to be no good reason to accept premise 5. On the contrary, it is natural to think that what is designated by a phrase of the form «S's causing E» is an event or episode that includes E as a part, as well as the causal relation between E and whatever S did to cause E; so S's causing R to become offended (by voting against a proposal) must be distinct from S's voting against a proposal, because the first has a part, R's becoming offended, that the second lacks. This is an intuition that we should give up only on the strength of a powerful argument against it.

But I have been repeatedly astonished to find proponents of the extreme minimizing view slipping identities like 5 into their reasoning without any argument at all, as if they were intuitively obvious. Consider, for example, the following remarks of Davidson's.

It will not help to think of [the queen's killing of the king by pouring poison in his ear] as an action that begins when the movement of the hand takes place but ends later. For . . . when we inquire into the relation between these events, the answer must be that the killing consists of the hand movement and one of its consequences. We can put them together in this way because the movement of the hand caused the death. But then, in moving her hand, the queen was doing something that caused the death of the king. . . . *Doing something that causes a death is identical with causing a death.* But there is no distinction to be made between causing the death of a person and killing him. It follows that what we thought was a more attenuated event

59

– the killing – took no more time, and did not differ from, the movement of the hand.[18]

The premise of Davidson's argument that I have italicized strikes me, prima facie, as highly deniable. This same assumption – that a designator of the form «*S*'s causing *E*» refers to the same event or action as does «*S*'s doing something that caused *E*» – is made at several places in Hornsby (1980). It puzzles me that these philosophers think this needs no argument. Perhaps they think that it follows from the truth-conditional equivalence between «*S* caused *E*» and «*S* did something that caused *E*». But of course, it does not follow, any more than "*S*'s eating exactly three doughnuts this morning = *S*'s eating her third and last doughnut of the morning" follows from the equivalence between "*S* ate exactly three doughnuts this morning" and "*S* ate her third and last doughnut of the morning".

Hornsby suggests another argument against premise 2 of the argument against temporal relations.[19] It goes like this: If *S*'s action of offending *R* by voting against a proposal included *R*'s becoming offended (or indeed, anything that occurred after *S*'s basic action by which she raised her hand), then that action would have to have been still going on at the time of *R*'s becoming offended; but (a) *S* did not *do* anything relevant after raising her hand; therefore, since (b) "any moment at which [*S*'s] action is occurring is a moment when *S* is doing something", *S*'s action could not have been still occurring at the time of *R*'s becoming offended and so could not have included the latter event as a part. This argument seems to me no better than the following one: Since any moment at which *S*'s typing *action* was occurring was a moment when *S* was typing *action,* and since *S* did not type *action* after *S* typed the first three letters of *action,* *S*'s typing *action* could not have been still occurring at the time of *S*'s typing the last three letters of *action,* and so could not have included the latter event as a part. The argument equivocates between two senses in which a time may be said to be one *when,* or *at which,* an event is occurring: (i) The time is wholly included in the total stretch of time occupied by the event; (ii) the time wholly includes the total stretch of time occupied by the event. From the proposition that *S* was not *doing* something at *t* in sense (ii) (no whole action of *S*'s occurred within *t*) – which is the sense in which

18 Davidson (1980, p. 58; emphasis added).
19 Hornsby (1980, p. 9).

Hornsby's premise (a) is true – it does not follow that *S* was not doing something at *t* in sense (i) (that no action of *S*'s had parts that occurred at *t*, as well as parts that occurred before *t*) – which is the sense in which Hornsby's premise (b) is true and not question begging. A somewhat similar equivocation occurs in Hornsby's remark that "once [*S*] has moved his arm, no *further* action is called for" in order for *S* to have operated the pump and replenished the water supply.[20] For this to be true, "further action" has to mean a wholly new and separate action that does not have *S*'s moving his arm as a part. But on that understanding, its truth is quite compatible with the claim that *S*'s operating the pump was a further action than *S*'s moving his arm, in the different sense that it included further parts than *S*'s moving his arm.

These arguments of Hornsby's are reminiscent of some remarks of Davidson's:

> Is it not absurd to suppose that, after the queen has moved her hand in such a way as to cause the king's death, any deed remains for her to do or to complete? She has done her work; it only remains for the poison to do its.[21]

> We never do more than move our bodies: the rest is up to nature.[22]

In these and in Hornsby's remarks, one can see a slightly different argument from the equivocating ones I exposed in the preceding paragraph. In its most general form, the argument is this: All *S* had to *do* in order to cause *E* was to perform her action that caused *E*; therefore, all *S* did, *S*'s only action, in causing *E* was her action that caused *E*. (For example, all *S* had to do in order to offend *R* [kill the king] was to move her hand; therefore, *S*'s only action in offending *R* [killing the king] was her moving her hand.) This is no better than the following argument: All that had to happen in order for that forest fire to happen was for those dry pine needles to catch fire; therefore, all that did happen, the only event, in that forest fire's happening was those dry pine needles catching fire. That is no good at all. Just as one event may be said to be sufficient for a larger event of which it is a part when it is sufficient in the circumstances for the other parts of that larger event, so one action may be said to be sufficient for a larger action of which it is a part when it is sufficient in the circumstances for the other parts of that action.

---

20 Hornsby (1980, p. 9; emphasis added).
21 Davidson (1980, p. 58).
22 Davidson (1980, p. 59).

Another thing that may lead some to assert identities like 5 earlier, and hence to deny premise 2 of the argument from temporal relations, is the following thought: To regard «S's causing E» as designating S's action that caused E, even though E occurred later than that action, is to do no more than we do when we regard "the birth of the thirty-fifth president of the United States" as designating an event that occurred on May 29, 1917, even though the person born then did not become president until 1960.[23] For the same sort of reason in both cases, it might be said, the designator succeeds in picking out a certain event only because there occurred a certain later event: The earlier event became one to which that designator applies only when the later event occurred. But the analogy is flawed. The cases are not relevantly similar. We can say that the thirty-fifth president of the United States was born in 1917, even though he became the thirty-fifth president much later. But we cannot say that S killed R yesterday, or that R was killed by S yesterday, if R did not die until today; we cannot say that S offended R this morning if it was not until this afternoon that R felt offense as a result of S's action this morning. We can say that the thirty-fifth president of the United States did not become president until some time after Rose Kennedy gave birth to the thirty-fifth president of the United States. We cannot say "R did not become offended until some time after S offended her" or "R did not die until some time after S killed R" or "The building's collapse did not occur until some time after the earthquake caused it to collapse".[24] Such data undermine the analogy used to support the claim that «S's causing E» designates S's action that caused E. In fact, they go against the claim itself.

There is further evidence against the claim. For instance, it is quite all right to say "The treatment is over, but we haven't cured him yet; we have to wait and see what effect it will have" or "If he dies, you will have killed him". On the other hand, there is the datum that "That blow may have killed him" *can* be used to mean that it may be that he will die as a result of the blow[25] (though we would be more comfortable with this form of words when the meaning

23 Bennett (1973) makes this suggestion.
24 Pointed out in Thomson (1971a), from which are drawn the last two examples. Thomson imagines a situation in which, if the denial of propositions like premise 2 were correct, someone could point to a still standing building and say truly, "There's our library. Unfortunately, an earthquake caused it to collapse yesterday."
25 As Thorp (1980, pp. 58–9) points out.

is that he may already have died as a result of the blow). But this is not really evidence that an action of killing can occur before the relevant death (or, more generally, an action of causing before the relevant effect). It is more like our saying "With that play he may have won the game" before the game is over, when it is clear that we mean that it may be that he *will* have won the game as a result of that play, rather than that he *has*, literally, won the game before it is over.

I have now considered all the arguments I know of against premise 2 of the argument from temporal relations and found none of them successful. So that premise, and with it the whole argument, remains compelling. It shows that designators like B.7 and B.8 designate different actions (provided that they designate actions at all: It is open to the extreme minimizer to admit that the temporal relations argument shows that designators like B.7 and B.8 designate different concrete events, but deny that they both designate actions, deny, in fact, that any but what I call basic action-designators designate actions).

The arguments for identities like 5 that we have considered (and rejected) are arguments that «S's causing E at t by V-ing at t^*» designates the same action as does «S's V-ing at t^*». These arguments could, in obvious ways, be converted to equally good arguments for the proposition that «S's V-ing in circumstance C» designates the same action as does «S's V-ing». Thus they are equally good arguments for the more general proposition that for any canonical action-designators X and Y such that X GEN Y, X and Y designate the same action, since, where the action designated by Y does not consist in that designated by X, X GEN Y holds only if Y designates an action because the action designated by X had a certain consequence or occurred in a certain circumstance. (The GEN relation, recall, is defined as follows: «S's U-ing at t^*» GEN «S's V-ing at t» if and only if [1] «S's V-ing at t» BY «S's U-ing at t^*», [2] «S's V-ing at t» is of the form «S's X-ing at t by U-ing at t^*», or [3] «S's V-ing at t» is of the form «S's U-ing at t^* in circumstance C» and is such that some action-designator has the BY relation to «S's U-ing at t^*» because it has the BY relation to it.) This means that these arguments, if successful, would show that every action-designator

63

designates the same action as some basic action-designator: They would *establish* the extreme minimizing thesis about individuation of actions, not merely rebut the temporal relations argument against it. But, as we have seen, these arguments are not successful.

There is another consideration that might be put forward in favor of the extreme minimizing view, namely, Occam's razor: Do not multiply actions beyond necessity. If, on the extreme minimizing account of what actions are, we can make as good sense of our ordinary action talk and as well formulate and discuss all the other questions about action that interest us, as we can on any more multiplicative account, then should we not adopt the account that minimizes the number of actions? Even supposing that the if-clause here is true (and the argument from temporal relations gives reason to doubt its first conjunct), this consideration has less weight than it may at first seem to have when one considers that minimizing the number of actions one posits is not the same as minimizing the number of *entities* one posits. The other views on action individuation give coherent accounts of the entities they say actions are, of such a nature as to make it clear that there are such entities, whether or not they are to be counted as actions. Once one understands what an exemplifying of an action property is, then one sees that there are such things, whether or not one agrees with Goldman that actions are always to be taken to be such things. And once one understands what I call *concrete* actions, then one will see (I hope) that there are such things, whether or not one agrees with me that these should be called actions. Moreover, the question as to whether either of these sorts of entities can be reduced to other sorts is independent of the question as to whether entities of these sorts are properly called actions. To adopt the extreme minimizing view, rather than one of the others, is not to minimize the number of entities one must suppose there are; it is only to restrict the term *action* to a narrower rather than a broader class of the entities there are. Thus this view does not really enjoy the sort of advantage we have in mind (or should have in mind) when we appeal to ontological parsimony.

We have considered all the *arguments* for the extreme minimizing view I know of, but they may not be the real source of the view. It may be that, quite apart from these arguments, extreme minimizers have a fundamental intuition that an action should not have parts that are not themselves actions, especially not parts whose occurrence is logically independent of the existence of the agent, such as a door's opening or the chair's having just called for the "no" votes. Not sharing this intuition, the rest of us need an argument for it, a better one than any I have found.

What is this sort of thing that I am calling a *concrete* action and that I say is what we commonly refer to when we refer to an action? I have said that it is more concrete, more determinate than the rather abstract sort of particular that Goldman calls an action, and I have talked about how a complex action is a layered structure comprising core action and outer layer(s) of consequence or circumstance. But that is not enough. To establish that there is a sort of thing I have in mind here, and what it is, I need to give a criterion of individuation for concrete actions. That is, I need to explain what is necessary and sufficient for it to be the case that two different canonical action-designators designate one and the same concrete action.

First, a reminder of the stipulations we have made about a *canonical* action-designator. A canonical action-designator has the form "S's V-ing at t", it picks out an action of S's uniquely, "V-ing" makes fully explicit the sort of action picked out (that is, the features that define the sort of action specified by the designator must be knowable solely on the basis of understanding the predicate "V"), and the consequence(s) or circumstance(s) comprising the outer layer(s) of the action are just those implied by the descriptive content of "V-ing".

It is obvious that two canonical action-designators designate the same action only if the agents they refer to are the same and the times they refer to overlap in such a way that the action designated by each designator occurred during the period of overlap. Let us call two canonical action-designators related in this way *co-agential* and *co-temporal*.

Our criterion for when two co-agential and co-temporal designators designate the same concrete action (rather than different concrete actions of the same agent at the same time) must reflect our notion of how an action is composed: Either an action is a simple mental act, or it is composed of an action as a core plus a layer of consequence or circumstance, or it is a conjunction of actions. We want the action designated by one designator to be the same as that designated by another, just in case it is clear, from the designators themselves, that the actions designated are built up in the same way from the same parts: Either the one is the same simple action as the other, or the one is composed of the same core action and the same layer of circumstance or consequence as the other, or the one is an aggregate of the same actions as the other. This last statement, though it casts some light on how concrete actions are individuated, does not give the criterion we want, because it makes use of the notion of same action in specifying what makes it the case that two designators designate the same action. We want a criterion that cites facts about the action-designators that are expressible without use of the notion of same action.

Given our idea of what a concrete action is, any pair of canonical action-designators that intuitively designate the same concrete action will fall into one or another of three classes. One obvious class comprises the pairs of *equivalent* designators, where «S's V-ing at t» is equivalent to «S's U-ing at $t^\star$» if and only if it is necessarily true that S V-ed at t if and only if S U-ed at $t^\star$. So, for example, «S's speaking a Finnish sentence at t» is equivalent to «S's uttering a sentence of Finnish at t», «S's just now rubbing her head and at the same time patting her stomach» is equivalent to «S's just now patting her stomach and simultaneously rubbing her head», and «S's typing b and then typing y at t» is equivalent to «S's typing y and before that typing b at t».

A second class of co-designating pairs contains those pairs of nonequivalent designators in which one designator details an aggregate of actions (say, «S's typing b and then typing y at t») and the other (say, «S's typing by at t») designates an action that *consisted in* that aggregate. The relation between the two designators in such a case I call the CONSISTED IN relation and define it this way: «S's V-ing at t» CONSISTED IN «S's U-ing at t» if and only if «S's V-ing at t consisted in S's U-ing at t» is true. As we noted earlier, this is one of the relations in virtue of which the BY relation holds. If X CONSISTED IN Y, then X BY Y: If S's typing by consisted in S's first typing b and then typing y, then, just because of that, S typed by by first typing b and then typing y.

In the third and last class are pairs of nonequivalent action-designators in which neither one details an aggregate of actions but both intuitively designate the same concrete action because one merely gives more or different information about intrinsic features of the action designated by the other. These are pairs such as «S's raising her hand at t» and «S's slowly raising her hand at t», or «S's shooting R at t» and «S's shooting R with a pistol at t», or «S's opening a door at t» and «S's opening a door at t by pushing it with her hand». In each of these pairs, the second designator, though obviously designating the same concrete action as the first, gives us more information of one kind or another about intrinsic features of the action: In the first pair, it is more information about the manner of the action; in the second pair, it is more information about the intrinsic nature of an instrument used in the action; in the third pair, it is more information about intrinsic properties of the method used in the action. And of course, there can be a pair in which *each* member gives information about some intrinsic feature of the manner, method, instrument, or bodily part used in the action that the other does not give, for example, the pair «S's raising her right hand at t» and «S's slowly raising her hand at t», or the pair «S's opening a door by pushing it at t» and «S's opening a door with her hand at t».

The criterion I propose is a disjunction of three conditions, one for each of the three classes just described:

> Given that X and Y are co-agential and co-temporal canonical action-designators, they designate the same action if and only if
> either
> (a) X is semantically equivalent to Y,
> (b) X CONSISTED IN Y, or
> (c) for every canonical action-designator Z, Z GEN X if and only if Z GEN Y.

It is obvious that a pair of canonical action-designators belongs to the first class I mentioned previously just in case it satisfies condition (a) and belongs to the second class just in case it satisfies condition (b). It is not so obvious that a pair belongs to the third class just in case it satisfies condition (c). But reflection on examples can make this clear.

Suppose that the following are canonical action-designators:

(1) «S's opening a red door at t»
(2) «S's slowly opening a door at t»
(3) «S's opening a door at t by pushing on it»

Intuitively, these designate the same concrete action. They simply give different, nonequivalent information about the manner or method of, or the intrinsic nature of things involved in, the same action. If a given action-designator has the GEN relation to any of these three, then it must have it to each of the others. For example, «S's pushing on a door at t» obviously has the BY relation to (3); equally obviously, it has the GEN relation also to (1) and (2) (given that each of [1] to [3] does uniquely designate an action). Suppose that «S's exerting a force with her hand at t» has the GEN relation to (1) (because «S opened a door by exerting force with her hand at t» is true). Then it also has it to (2) and (3) (because «S slowly opened a door by exerting force with her hand at t» and «S opened a door by pushing on it, by exerting force with her hand, at t» are both true). Suppose that «S's continually exerting a slight force with her hand over the period $t^\star$» has the GEN relation to (2) (because «at t, S slowly opened a door by continually exerting a slight force with her hand over the period $t^\star$» is true). Then it has the GEN relation also to (1) and (3) (because «at t, S opened a door by continually exerting a slight force with her hand over the period $t^\star$» and «at t, S opened a door by pushing on it, by continually exerting a slight force with her hand over the period $t^\star$» are both true). We get the same sort of results if in any of (1) to (3) we replace "hand" with "right hand" and "door" with "heavy door", or if in (3) we modify "pushing" with "slowly": Any canonical action-designator will have the GEN relation to any of (1) to (3) if and only if it has it to all the others.

The preceding paragraph argued that a pair of action-designators in the third class mentioned earlier, which satisfies neither (a) nor (b), must satisfy (c). To convince yourself of the converse, that a pair satisfying neither (a) nor (b) satisfies (c) only if it is in the third class, try to think of a counterexample. Try to think of another reason why a nonequivalent pair of action-designators, where neither CONSISTS IN the other, would be such that they are action-generated by all the same action-designators, other than the reason that they merely give different information about the intrinsic features of the same action (its manner or method or instrument). I think you can't do it.[26]

26 David Widerker (personal communication) has asked whether the following would be a counterexample here: Suppose that explosives in two different houses were wired to a single button in such a way that by pressing that button once at t, I blew up both houses. Now consider the following action-designators:

X: my blowing up house 1 at t;
Y: my blowing up house 2 at t.

X and Y do not designate the same concrete action, but do they not satisfy condition (c) of my criterion? (Condition [c] was: For every canonical action-

Note, by the way, that although a pair of action-designators not satisfying (a) or (b) must satisfy (c) if they designate the same action, such a pair of designators need not satisfy the reverse of condition (c), namely, «for all Z, X GEN Z if and only if Y GEN Z», in order to designate the same action. Recall the example in which S offended R by voting against R's proposal. Let X be «S's raising her hand *slowly* when the "no" votes were called for», let Y be «S's raising her hand when the "no" votes were called for», and let Z be «S's giving R some comfort». Here, though X and Y designate the same concrete action, X GEN Z but not Y GEN Z because Z BY X but not Z BY Y. S gave R some comfort by raising her hand *slowly* when the "no" votes were called for, but it is not the case that S gave R some comfort by raising her hand when the "no" votes were called for.

Such examples show that sometimes what is designated by the *right*-hand relatum of the BY relation must be taken to be an exemplifying of an act property rather than a concrete action. It is never the case, however, that the *left*-hand relatum must be so taken. If S moved a lever slowly at t by continually exerting a slight force with her hand over the period $t^\star$, then S moved a lever at t by continually . . . and so on; and if S moved a lever at t by exerting force with her hand at t, then S moved a lever slowly at t by exerting force with her hand at t. The BY relation can force its right-hand relatum to be interpreted as designating an exemplifying of a property rather than a concrete action when the BY relation holds in virtue of a causal relation between what is designated by its right-hand relatum and some event or state of affairs; as we observed earlier, sometimes causal explanations can force this understanding of one or the other

designator Z, Z GEN X if and only if Z GEN Y.) Is there any action-designator Z that has the GEN relation to one of X and Y but not to the other? The action-designator «my pressing the button at t» obviously has the GEN relation to both X and Y, for it has the BY relation to both X and Y. And so, any designator that has the GEN relation to that designator thereby has the GEN relation to both X and Y.

True enough, but notice that, given the fact that my single pressing of the button blew up both houses, one can say that by blowing up house 1 by pressing that button, I also blew up house 2, (and vice versa: By blowing up house 2 by pressing that button, I blew up house 1). But one cannot say that by blowing up house 1 by pressing that button, I blew up house 1 (any more than one can say that by blowing up house 1, I blew up house 1). So an action-designator that has the BY and hence the GEN relation to Y but not to X is «my blowing up house 1 by pressing the button at t».

of their relata. But in such a case, when the BY relation holds because of what the action designated by its right-hand relatum has caused, what was caused is never identical to (but is always only a part of) the action designated by the left-hand relatum. That is why it is only the right-hand and never the left-hand relatum of the BY relation that can be forced to be taken as designating an exemplifying of an action property rather than a concrete action.

(Note also that conditions [b] and [c] are mutually exclusive. If action-designators X and Y satisfy [b], then they do not satisfy [c]; and, hence, by contraposition, if they satisfy [c], then they do not satisfy [b]. This holds because if [b] X CONSISTS IN Y then X BY Y; but if X BY Y then X and Y do not satisfy [c], because there is an action-designator that has the GEN relation to X but not to Y, namely, Y itself, for no action-designator has the GEN relation to itself.)

CONCLUDING CAVEAT

I have completed my account of concrete actions and their individuation. But before I leave this topic, I should confess that it seems to me that the issue over the individuation of action, though sufficiently interesting in its own right, is not one on which much else depends. As far as I can see, there is no other significant question in the philosophy of action that depends on it. Whichever account one adopts, one can equally well state and discuss the metaphysical questions about action that the present book addresses in its other chapters (What is the general mark of action? What is it for action to be intentional? Is free action compatible with determinism? What makes a reasons explanation of an action true?), and one can equally well defend any of the serious answers to them.

The dispute about individuation of actions is not much more than a verbal issue. None of the three accounts we have considered – the extreme maximizing account of Goldman (which takes actions to be exemplifyings of action properties), the extreme minimizing account of Anscombe, Davidson, and Hornsby (which takes actions to be basic actions), and my middling account (which takes actions to be what I call *concrete actions*) – is more ontologically parsimonious than the others: They disagree only about which of the things there are are properly called actions. Moreover, any of the three accounts can be made to work in the sense that, first, each can be spelled out well enough so that one can see that it gives a coherent account of the kind of thing it says actions must be, and, second, each can find *some* support in our ordinary talk about actions. Though my concrete actions account is, I hope to have shown, better supported, it refines and regiments what is meant by an action beyond anything demonstrable from our ordinary talk. If there are reasons for preferring that account, they are reasons, not so much for a judgment as to what we already plainly mean by an action, but for a decision as to what more precise thing we should mean when precision about the individuation of actions is called for.

4

Intentional action

Some actions are intentional and some are not. For example, Sarah's action of stepping on Susy's toes was not intentional, but Susy's subsequent action of stepping on Sarah's toes was intentional. Whether an action was intentional or not can be important. It can make a difference in our attitude toward the action and in our evaluation of it. What makes an action intentional? Let me rephrase the question. Given that «S's V-ing at t» is a canonical designator of an action, what is necessary and sufficient for the truth of «S's V-ing at t was intentional (SV-ed at t intentionally)»?

The same action can be intentional under one designator of it and not intentional under another. For example, «S's pirouetting at t» and «S's pirouetting clumsily at t» designate the same action. But it may nevertheless be correct to say that S's pirouetting was intentional but S's pirouetting *clumsily* was not intentional.

Some canonical action-designators *imply* that the action they designate was intentional (at least under that designation), for example, «S's calling for help at t», «S's looking around her at t», «S's groping for the light switch at t», «S's deciding to run away at t», «S's mentally saying "nonsense" at t», or any of the form «S's intentionally V-ing at t». Other designators imply that the designated action was *not* intentional (at least under that designation), for example, any of the form «S's unintentionally V-ing at t». Still other designators imply neither that the action designated was intentional nor that it was not intentional, for example, «S's raising her arm at t», «S's knocking over a vase at t», «S's pressing a button at t», «S's opening a door at t», and «S's (voluntarily) exerting force forward with her hand at t». Call designators in this last class *neutral*. If «S's V-ing at t» is a neutral designator, then it will not be redundant to add to it either of the modifiers "intentionally" or "not intentionally".

Recall that, according to the definition given at the end of Chapter 1, an action is either simple (clause [i] of the definition), complex (clause [ii]), or an aggregate of simple or complex actions (clause [iii]). Simple actions are all mental actions and include, most importantly, volitions. Voluntary exertions of the body and actions done by voluntarily exerting the body are complex; that is, they are structures consisting of a simpler core action (by doing which the agent does the larger complex action) and a consequence or circumstance of it (that is usually not an action). Thus, for example, S's firing a gun (on a certain occasion) was a complex action composed of S's pulling a trigger, as its core action, plus the consequence of the gun's firing; S's violating a city ordinance on that occasion was also a complex action consisting in S's firing a gun within the city limits, as its core action, plus the circumstance that there was an ordinance prohibiting firing of guns within the city limits. Thus there can be nested groups of actions in which one action is the core of a more complex action, which in turn is the core of a still more complex action, and so on. The canonical designators of the actions in such a nested group form what in Chapter 3 we called an action tree. The following list, for example, is an action tree.

1. S's willing to exert a certain force in a certain direction with her finger at t.
2. S's (voluntarily) exerting that force in that direction with her finger at t.
3. S's pulling a trigger at t.
4. S's firing a gun at t.
5. S's firing a gun within the city limits at t.
6. S's violating a city ordinance at t.

Here each succeeding action was done by doing the preceding one and is composed of the preceding one plus some consequence or circumstance of it. The first action, a volition, is the only simple, basic action on the list, and it is the ultimate core of every later action on the list.

Any simple, basic action (which, according to me, must be a mental action) is intentional by its very nature. S's deciding to run away could not fail to be intentional, nor could S's mentally saying *nonsense*, nor could S's forming a mental image of her girlhood home (if it was an action). Nor could a volition not be intentional. Given any canonical designator of a simple, basic action, it will not make sense to add "not intentionally" to it. It is not that simple, basic actions must always be *accompanied* by intentions to perform them (or otherwise they would not be actions). It is, rather, that simple, basic actions are intrinsically intentional actions. (Analogously, integers are intrinsically rational numbers.) The possibility of failing to be intentional (and thus the possibility of having a neutral designator) comes in only with complex actions, only when an action contains a layer of consequence or circumstance that the agent could conceivably fail to expect or fail to be aware of when performing the core action.

COMPLEX ACTIONS

Suppose that «*S*'s *V*-ing at *t*» is a neutral designator of a complex action. What is necessary and sufficient for the truth of «*S*'s *V*-ing at *t* was *intentional*»? One thing is obvious: A complex action will be intentional only if it has a simpler core action that is intentional. Given a complex action that is intentional, you must be able, by peeling off layers of consequence or circumstance, to come to a core action that is also intentional. Of course, ultimately you will come to its basic core, which, being a simple mental action, is intrinsically intentional. But typically, many of the nonbasic, simpler core actions will be intentional. My action of putting an asterisk on the computer screen was intentional, and so was my action of pressing the key by which I put it there, and so was my action of exerting force downward with my finger by which I pressed the key, and so on.[1] (Also, from the fact that an action was *not* intentional, one often infers that a larger action of which it was a core was not intentional. Since *S*'s pulling of the trigger was *not* intentional, then neither was her thereby firing the gun nor her thereby firing it within the city limits nor her thereby violating a city ordinance.) But the important point for our purposes is the necessary one: No complex intentional action can fail to have some simpler intentional action as a core.

Given that a core action is intentional, what else is needed to make a complex action intentional? It is clear that something more

---

1 As David Widerker has pointed out to me, it is not the case that every core action of an intentional complex action must be intentional. For example, by causing certain electronic events inside the computer I intentionally put an asterisk on the screen, but if I know nothing at all about the computer's internal workings, I do not intentionally cause those electronic events inside the computer.

is needed. Consider the nested group of actions listed in the previous section. The first action in the group is a simple, basic act of volition and therefore must have been intentional; but the intentionality might have stopped there or at any action further down the list. Although S exerted force with her finger by willing to do so, she might have actually exerted the force unintentionally if she firmly believed that her hand was paralyzed. Or S might have intentionally exerted the force with her finger, but thereby unintentionally pulled the trigger, if she believed that her finger was not near the trigger. Or S might have intentionally pulled the trigger, but thereby unintentionally fired the gun, if she believed that the gun was not loaded. And so on. Some further relation between the core action and the larger action (besides its being the core of that larger action) is required in order to transfer the intentionality of the core action to the larger action.

Let us lay out the shape of the condition on complex actions as we have it so far: If «S's V-ing at t» neutrally designates a complex action then «S's V-ing at t was intentional (under that description)» is true if and only if the following is true: «S's V-ing at t consisted in some action, S's A-ing at t, plus that action's causing certain results or occurring in certain circumstances, where

(a) S's A-ing at t was intentional, and
(b) S's A-ing at t had the right sort of relation to S's V-ing at t».

Our chief remaining task is to say what this right sort of relation is.

INTENTIONALLY DOING SOMETHING REQUIRES ONLY THE BELIEF COMPONENT OF INTENDING TO DO IT

At first blush, it may seem that for this relation to obtain, it is necessary that S intended of her intentional A-ing at t that she would thereby V. So, for instance, when S fired the gun by pulling the trigger, her firing the gun was intentional only if her pulling the trigger was accompanied by her intending of it that she would thereby fire the gun; S violated a city ordinance intentionally only if S intended of her firing the gun within the city limits that she would thereby violate a city ordinance. But reflection shows, surprisingly, that such claims need not always be true, that we cannot make the intention to V a necessary condition of V-ing intentionally.[2]

2 I became persuaded of this by Bratman (1987, ch. 8).

There are two rather different sorts of cases that show this. One sort, which occurs commonly, is illustrated by the following examples. As I start my noisy car early one morning, I am aware that I am almost certainly thereby disturbing the sleep of some people in nearby houses. I need not, however, *intend* to disturb their sleep. It need not be any part of my *plans* to do so. I need not be committed to disturbing their sleep, as an end or as a means to some further end, in the way that intending to do such a thing would require. If I somehow learned that my starting the car would not after all disturb anyone's sleep, I would not on that account feel that any of my plans or intentions would be in any way frustrated; I would not think that I would either have to seek other ways of disturbing their sleep or else abandon one of my intentions. As I start my car, however, I do know that almost certainly I will thereby wake some neighbors, and that means that, if I do wake some of them, I do so intentionally, despite my neither intending nor wanting to do this. If a neighbor later said to me, "You knew how noisy your car is, and you knew people were sleeping nearby; you *intentionally* woke us up at that ungodly hour", I could not deny the justice of the accusation, its implication as to the sort of responsibility I bear for waking them. I could not get out of it by pleading that I did not *intend* to wake them. Similarly, if in giving hard use to a broom I borrowed I wore it down considerably, I could not parry the accusation that I wore it down intentionally by pleading that wearing it down was never something I intended or wanted to do.[3] In general, side effects of an intended action that the agent *expects* (in the sense that she is aware at the time of choosing the action that she will or might thereby bring them about) need not therefore be effects the agent *intends* to bring about, but they are therefore effects she brings about intentionally.

The other sort of case of *V*-ing while lacking the intention to *V* is not so common.[4] Here is an example. I confront a set of double doors through which I wish to go. I know that the doors open only one way, either toward me or away from me, but I do not know

---

3 As Bratman (1987) says (p. 124), "An important role played by our . . . classifying actions as intentional is that of identifying [actions] for which an agent may be held responsible." Bratman quotes a remark from Sidgwick (1907, p. 202): "we cannot evade responsibility for any foreseen bad consequence of our acts by the plea that we felt no desire for them."

4 Bratman (1984) was, as far as I know, the first to note this sort of case of *V*-ing intentionally while lacking the intention to *V*.

which. I am in a hurry, so I simultaneously push away from me on one of the doors and pull toward me on the other. Suppose that I open the door I push on. In pushing on it I am trying to push it open, and I succeed. So I open it intentionally. If it were the other door, the one I pull on, that opened, then I would open *it* intentionally. But for neither door can we say that I have the intention to open it. We cannot suppose that I have *both* intentions, the intention to push open the one door and the intention to pull open the other, for it would be quite irrational of me to intend to accomplish both of these ends while knowing that it is impossible to do so. But it is not irrational of me to *try* both courses of action simultaneously while knowing that at most one can succeed, given that I do not know which one will succeed. And it would be arbitrary to attribute one of the intentions to me rather than the other. Therefore, neither intention can be attributed to me.

To put the lesson in general terms, an agent can rationally undertake two (or more) courses of action aimed at separate ends such that she knows she can achieve at most one of those ends and therefore does not, if she is rational, intend to achieve all of them. The content of her intention is only the disjunction of the alternative ends and not any one alternative by itself. If she succeeds in achieving one of the ends, then she achieves it intentionally, despite lacking the intention to achieve it.

In both sorts of cases we have considered, of V-ing intentionally while lacking the intention to V, it is necessary for S's having V-ed intentionally that S was aware at the time of undertaking her action that she would or might thereby V: S committed herself to acting in full knowledge that V-ing was among the things she would or might thereby do. It is this expectation, instead of the stronger condition that she intended of her action that she thereby V, that is necessary for her having V-ed intentionally. Her having this expectation would be entailed if S did have that intention, and it is the only belief about her V-ing that is entailed by her having that intention. No belief that she *will* thereby V, no stronger belief than that she *might* thereby V, is required. This is nicely shown by Donald Davidson's example of his intentionally making a tenth carbon copy while both intending to do so and being uncertain that he is succeeding in doing so.[5] (In a case where S did intend to V, one might

5 Davidson (1980, p. 92).

put the entailed weak expectation this way: S believed that there was at least enough chance of her V-ing to make it worth the effort to try.)

One necessary ingredient of the relation that we are seeking to define, between the core action and the larger complex action, is this: At *t*, S believed of her *A*-ing that she would or might thereby *V*. Is this, when added to the intentionality of S's *A*-ing at *t*, sufficient to make S's *V*-ing at *t* intentional? Unfortunately, it is not. Here are some counterexamples:

1. S entered the room, intending thereby to enter it after the queen entered, and she did so. But this was completely a matter of luck, for the person S saw entering the room just before she did, whom S believed to be the queen, was not in fact the queen. It seems that S *accidentally,* not intentionally, entered the room after the queen.
2. S voted for the motion by intentionally moving her right hand over her head and touching her left ear with her right index finger, and S intended of her moving her right hand, and so on, that she would thereby vote for the motion. But it was completely a matter of luck that she did so. For the relevant rules dictate that what actually counts as voting for the motion is raising your right elbow above shoulder height, whereas S thought that all that was required is that one touch one's left ear with one's right index finger. It therefore seems wrong to say that she voted for the motion intentionally.
3. "Here is an example of Daniel Bennett's. A man may try to kill someone by shooting at him. Suppose the killer misses his victim by a mile, but the shot stampedes a herd of wild pigs that trample the intended victim to death. Do we want to say the man killed his victim *intentionally*?" (From Davidson, 1980, p. 78)

Example 3 presents what has come to be called the *problem of wayward causal chains*. Not just any causal connection between an intentional action and an expected, or even intended, result makes producing that result intentional. The causal chain must follow the right sort of route. Examples 1 and 2 show there are other problems here besides that of unlooked-for *causal chains,* and we will soon see further such examples. But first, let us have two more examples of wayward causal chains:

4. S came into a room in a new building and flipped a light switch on the wall, intending thereby to turn on the overhead light in the room. That

particular switch, however, was not yet connected to the light. But a switch on the other side of the room was connected, and R, who was standing near this latter switch, flipped it because he saw S flip the switch that R knew to be unconnected. So S's intentional flipping of the switch caused the light to go on and S intended it to have that result, but surely S's causing the light to go on was not intentional.

5. S was playing soccer and had the ball not far from the opponent's goal. She delivered a hard kick to the ball, intending thereby to cause the ball to go into the goal. But the route the ball took was remarkably circuitous: It came off the side of S's foot and hit the shoulder of a defending player, whence it bounced back toward the center of the field and hit the back of another defending player, whence it rebounded back toward and into the goal. S caused the ball to go into the goal by kicking it, and that was something she expected and intended to do. But S did not do this in such a way that we can say that her doing it was intentional.

Examples 1 to 5 suggest that we might get a condition that is sufficient for the relation we are trying to define if we add to the necessary condition already given the following: At t, what S believed of her A-ing about *how* she would thereby V was not false of how S actually did thereby V. Unfortunately, what we then get is not necessary for the relation we are trying to define. There are possible cases of intentional action that do not satisfy it:

6. S had the soccer ball fairly close to the opponents' goal. She had a wide opening to the goal and kicked the ball hard, believing that by doing so she would cause it to go straight over the ground and into the goal, untouched by any other player. But the opposing goal tender made a surprisingly quick, long horizontal lunge and managed to touch the ball with her extended hand, thus deflecting it slightly from a straight path, but not nearly enough to cause it to miss the goal. It does *not* seem that *this* unexpected deflection makes it wrong to say that S kicked the ball into the goal intentionally.

7. S entered a room she had not been in before, and saw an ordinary-looking light suspended from the ceiling and an ordinary-looking light switch on the wall. She flipped the switch, intending thereby to turn on the light, and she believed that the way in which the switch flipping would cause the light to go on was through the usual mechanism of closing a wire circuit that includes the switch, a power source, and the light. But in fact, the mechanism by which the switch operated was different: It sent a radio signal to a receiver in the light fixture, which then activated a tiny generator to which the light was already connected. It does not seem that this mistaken belief as to how, by flipping the switch, she would turn on the light makes it wrong to say that S turned it on intentionally.

Moreover, there are examples that give reason to doubt that the conjunction of the two conditions is, after all, *sufficient* for the relation we are trying to define, examples of actions that satisfy it but do not seem to be intentional:

8. S entered a room, intending thereby to enter after the queen did. She believed correctly that the queen had already entered. This belief was not based on any false belief, but it *was* totally unjustified: She had no reason at all for holding it. Can her entering after the queen have been any less accidental, any more intentional, than in example 1?
9. In the park, S saw on the slope below her a small, riderless wagon rolling and gathering speed as it went toward a small child lying asleep on a blanket. In her panic, S shouted "Stop!" in the direction of the wagon, hoping that by doing so she would stop it. S had no belief as to how that shout could stop the wagon, just a desperate hope that somehow it might. Unknown to her, the wagon was remotely controlled by someone standing out of her sight, who saw her, heard her shout, and consequently stopped it. So, by shouting "Stop!", she caused it to stop, with the intention of thereby doing so and without any false belief as to how she would thereby do so, but did she do so intentionally?

In examples 8 and 9, our intuition goes against saying that the action was intentional; yet in neither example has the agent any false belief as to how her intentional core action will bring about the intended result.

Is there a general way of accounting for our intuitions regarding all of the examples considered so far? I think so. Examples 1 to 9 all fit the following form of description: S V-ed by A-ing; S A-ed intentionally and expected of her A-ing that she would or might thereby V. It seems right to say that for those examples where, despite this, S's V-ing failed to be intentional (examples 1 to 5, 8, and 9), but for none of them where it was intentional (examples 6 and 7), it was *too much of a lucky accident* that S V-ed by A-ing, given the *way* in which she V-ed by A-ing. Too lucky for what? Well, too lucky for S to get the same credit or blame, to have the same responsibility, for V-ing that would be appropriate had S V-ed intentionally. What guides our intuition in these cases about whether S's V-ing was intentional or not is the connection between that judgment and our judgment as to the credit (positive or negative) S deserves for V-ing: In example 6, S can legitimately claim credit for and take pride in having kicked the ball into the goal, but in example 7, S should merely feel lucky.

Our talk of luck here can be replaced by something more illuminating. What we are talking about has to do with how what actually happened relates to what S *was justified in believing* would happen.

Examples 8 and 9 show that, in addition to just believing of her intentional A-ing that she would or might thereby V, S must have some justification for this belief. If those examples do not convince you of that, try the following thought experiment. First, imagine an example where S intentionally A-ed and thereby V-ed but did not believe at all that she would or might thereby V. Suppose that S pressed what looked like a light switch button on the wall of her hotel room and, to her enormous surprise, thereby blew up the bed in the room next door. (The switch had been installed by a previous occupant of the room as part of an assassination plot.) In that case, of course, S's blowing up the bed next door (by intentionally pressing the button) was not intentional. Now imagine the case altered just in the respect that when S pressed the button (A-ed), she *imagined* that she would thereby blow up the bed next door (V) in just the way that she in fact did. Suppose that S had just been reading a fictional thriller in which someone was assassinated in that way. It is clear that that change does not make her blowing up the bed next door intentional. Now suppose the case changed just a bit more. Instead of merely imagining that her pressing the button would blow up the bed next door, she believed, *entirely without justification*, that it would do so: the imagining transformed somehow into an entirely unjustified belief (here it helps to suppose that S is a child). Does this alteration in the case change it from one where S's blowing up the bed next door was not intentional to one where it *was* intentional? Surely not. The mere belief without any justification, just like the mere imagining of a possibility, is insufficient to make the action intentional.

Our earlier examples show us something about what sort of justification for the belief is required. In the examples where S's V-ing was not intentional, despite S's believing that she would or might V by her A-ing and her having some justification for this belief (1 to 5), what justification S had was also at the same time justification for believing a *false* proposition about *how* she would V by A-ing. On the other hand, in the examples where S's V-ing was intentional, despite the fact that she did not V by A-ing in quite the way she expected to (6 and 7), S had good reason to believe the subjunctive conditional proposition that, *even if* she were not to V by A-ing in just the way she expected, she would nevertheless V by A-ing in one or another of a certain range of other ways, a conditional whose consequent turned out to be true.

81

In example 6, *S* had justification in what she then knew about her situation for believing that, even if the ball were not to go straight in but were to be somehow deflected off a straight course by another player, it might nevertheless go in by a nearly straight path as a result of her kick. This latter is *true* of how she kicked it in. By contrast, in example 5, where *S*'s kicking the ball into the goal was *not* intentional because the ball's route was so wayward, *S* had justification for believing pretty much the same thing as in example 6: that the chances were good that, even if it did not go straight in, it would still go in by a nearly direct route. But here this is *false* of how she kicked it in. In having justification for this false proposition, she did thereby have justification for a true, but less specific, proposition about how she would kick it in – that her kicking it would cause it to travel some path or other that led into the goal. But, and this is important, the *only* way in which she had justification for that nonspecific truth was through having justification for the more specific falsehood.

In example 7, in the fact that the switch she flipped looked so much like an ordinary light switch, *S* had some justification for believing that, even if the switch did not control the light by the sort of mechanism she was familiar with, it was set up to turn the light on and off by some sort of standing mechanism. And, of course, what justifies *that* truth about how her flipping the switch would cause the light to go on is not what justifies the (more specific) falsehood that it would cause it via the sort of mechanism she is familiar with. This contrasts with example 4, where the proposition that the switch flipping would cause the light to go on via some sort of standing mechanism is false, but it is only what justifies *S* in believing that falsehood that justifies her in believing the less specific truth that her flipping the switch would *somehow* cause the light to go on.

So we might propose the following as a second necessary condition for the relation we are trying to define: At *t*, *S* had justification for believing of her *A*-ing that she would or might thereby *V*, which was not at the same time justification for believing a proposition that was false of how she was actually going thereby to *V*. Let me give one more example to help explain what this statement means. Suppose that in a laboratory there is a setup whereby one pours liquid into a certain opening and it travels via one or the other but not both of two channels, *A* and *B*, to a certain vessel *C*. A switching gate at the forking of the channels determines which one the liquid goes through. There is a filter in each of the two channels, and this arrangement allows the whole setup to be used while one or the other filter is being cleaned. It is a strict rule of the laboratory that the open channel must always have a filter in it. S poured some liquid into the top opening. The lab assistant had just told S that he was in the process of cleaning the filter from channel B, but in fact it was the filter from channel A that he was cleaning. So S had justification for the false belief that by pouring the liquid into the apparatus, she would cause it to go through a filter in channel A to vessel C. But this did not prevent her action of causing the liquid to be filtered into vessel C from being intentional, because in her knowledge of the setup and of the laboratory rule, she had justification for believing the less specific but true proposition that by pouring the liquid into the apparatus she would cause it to go to vessel C through a filter in one channel or the other; and that justification for this truth was *not* justification for any falsehood about how she would accomplish that end.

FURTHER REFINEMENTS ON
THE RIGHT SORT OF RELATION

This second condition (concerning what S was justified in believing about how she would V by A-ing) together with the first condition (that S expected that she would or might V by A-ing) makes a conjunction that is sufficient for the relation we are trying to define, the relation such that a complex action is intentional if and only if one of its core actions has this relation to it and is itself intentional. Unfortunately, this second condition seems not quite *necessary* for intentional action.

There are two respects in which it falls short. One is seen in the following example. S is the field goal kicker on a football team (in the North American sense of "football"). In a game, S was called on to try for a field goal from fairly far out, near the maximum distance S had ever, even in practice, managed to kick the ball through the goal. On this occasion, when S kicked the ball, an unexpected gust of wind carried it between the goal posts above the crossbar; without the help of the wind, the ball would have fallen a few feet short. So far in the game there had been no significant wind and, as he kicked the ball, S had no reason at all to think that his kick would be aided by wind. So any justification S had for thinking that his kicking the ball would or might cause it to go between the goal posts above the crossbar was justification for thinking that it would or might do this without any assistance from wind, and that proposition is false of how it actually did this. Yet I am strongly inclined to say that S kicked the ball over the crossbar intentionally in this case. That is, I am inclined to say that this is so *provided* that S did not get *too much* help from the wind, provided that the ball would still have come fairly close even if there had been no gust of wind; if I suppose that the ball would have fallen twenty yards short if there had been no wind, then my inclination to regard S's kicking it over the crossbar as intentional disappears. How far short is too far? How much assistance from the wind is too much? Here again there comes into play the tie between our judgment about the intentionality of an action and our judgment about the credit the agent deserves for it. Too much assistance from the wind is enough to make the ball's going over too lucky for S to deserve the credit for causing it to go over that he would deserve had his doing so been intentional. This situation must, of course, be left rather vague: In this context, if the ball would have made it within one or two feet without the wind's assistance, then that assistance was not too much, but if the ball would have fallen several yards short, then the wind definitely did help too much.

We can protect against this sort of counterexample by an insubstantial amendment to our second condition. Merely replace "false proposition" with "proposition too far from the truth", so that the condition reads: At t, S had justification for believing of her A-ing that she might thereby V that was not, at the same time, justification for believing a proposition too far from the truth as to how she was actually going thereby to V.

With this revision, we are closer to a necessary condition for the intentionality of S's V-ing at t, but we are still not quite there, as is shown by an example given by George Wilson:

I might intend to execute Phipps in a chamber with lethal gas but, although I know better, I let it slip my mind that, because the gas reservoir has not been restocked, there is no gas for the lever to release. As I approach the chamber door, I accidentally and unwittingly strike the valve that fills the reservoir with my elbow and turn it on. When I do pull the lever a couple of minutes later, the chamber has been readied for operation and I kill my victim as I had expected to do . . . it seems to me that I intentionally kill

Phipps even though . . . I was not, in this situation, justified in believing that my act would kill him and it was only through a crucial accident that my act resulted in his death.[6]

I am inclined to agree with Wilson's intuition here that I do in this case intentionally kill Phipps. Why does the case strike me this way despite the fact that what I know – which includes the temporarily forgotten fact that the gas chamber was empty and I have not re-stocked it – does *not* justify me in believing that by pulling the lever I will or might kill Phipps? I think that the reason is this: It is only my knowledge of those facts that have slipped my mind that de-prives me of the relevant justification, so that if I had *failed to know those facts at all* (and not merely lost sight of them temporarily), then I *would* have had justification in what I knew for my true belief that by pulling the lever I would kill Phipps by releasing poison gas into the chamber; and this justification would not be justification for any false belief as to how I would kill Phipps by pulling the lever. Their slipping my mind at the crucial time makes these facts as irrelevant to the intentionality of my killing Phipps, and to the blame or credit I deserve for it, as if I had never known them.

(But, one may wonder, *why* would they not be relevant then? Suppose that, all along, I had justification for believing the false proposition that there was gas in the reservoir before I approached the chamber door and, while doing so, accidentally and unwittingly caused the reservoir to be restocked with gas. We would neverthe-less regard my killing Phipps by pulling the lever as intentional, as deserving of the same blame or credit, as it would have been if that false belief had been true. Why? It is because that false proposition is *not* a proposition *about how I would kill Phipps* and does not entail any false proposition about that act. My holding that false belief is therefore no more relevant to the intentionality of my killing Phipps than, say, my holding false beliefs about who built the execution chamber or what it is made of.)

Wilson's example shows the need for a further modification of our condition concerning what S was justified in believing about how she would V by A-ing. We need to insert just before "S had justification" the words "in what S knew that had not then slipped her mind", so that the condition now reads: At *t*, in what S knew that had not then slipped her mind, S had justification for this belief

6 Wilson (1980, pp. 118–19).

that was not, at the same time, justification for believing a proposition too far from the truth as to how she was actually going thereby to V.

With this change, we have a condition that is necessary for the intentionality of S's V-ing at t, and we have all the ingredients for the definition we have been seeking. It goes like this: S's A-ing at t had the right sort of relation to S's V-ing at t if and only if (1) at t, S believed of her A-ing that she would or might thereby V and (2) at t, in what S knew that had not then slipped her mind, S had justification for this belief that was not, at the same time, justification for believing a proposition too far from the truth as to how she was actually going thereby to V. As far as I can see now, these two conditions capture everything more that is necessary for the intentionality of a complex action, beyond the intentionality of its core action.

AGGREGATE ACTIONS

We have now given an account of intentionality for simple and complex actions. It remains only to say something about actions that are conjunctions or aggregates of actions. For example, the action of simultaneously rubbing one's stomach and patting one's head is a conjunction of two actions. The action of typing a sentence is an aggregate of several successive actions of typing individual letters. It is obvious that such an aggregate action is intentional only if each of its component actions is intentional. But this is not sufficient. S might have intentionally typed the letter b and then intentionally typed the letter y, as it happened right after the b, and so typed the sequence of letters by. But it is compatible with this that S did not believe of either of these actions that it would or might be part of her typing that sequence. It could have been that when S typed b she had no expectation of typing y, and when S typed y she had no memory of having typed b, in which case S would not have typed the sequence by intentionally. So it is also necessary that S believed of each of her V-ing's component actions, as she performed it, that it would or might be part of her V-ing.

But this is still not enough. For the conditions stated so far would be satisfied if S had typed b, expecting later to type y next to it, and later, having forgotten that she typed b, S typed y (as it happened, immediately to the right of the b), expecting later to type b in front of it. At that point, S had typed the sequence *by,* but not intentionally, despite having typed each letter intentionally and having believed of each of these single-letter typings that it would or might be part of her typing the sequence *by.* What is missing here and must, I believe, be required if the aggregate action was intentional is this: As S performed each component action of her V-ing, S was aware of or remembered those other component actions that were occurring at the same time or had already occurred (if there were any such), and believed of it and of them that they would or might be parts of her V-ing.

So what we need to say is this: If «S's V-ing at t» designates an aggregate of actions, then «S's V-ing at t was intentional» is true if and only if each component action was intentional and of each component action the following is true: «When S performed it, S believed of it and of the other component actions already performed or being performed that they would or might be parts of her V-ing».

THE FINAL, WHOLE DEFINITION

Putting all our results together, we have the following recursive definition of what makes an action intentional: Given that «S's V-ing at t» is a canonical designator of an action, «S's V-ing at t was *intentional*» is true if and only if either

(1) «S's V-ing at t» designates a simple action,
(2) It designates a complex action of which the following is true: «S's V-ing at t consists of some action, S's A-ing at t, plus that action's causing certain results or its occurring in certain circumstances, where
    (a) S's A-ing at t was intentional and
    (b) (i) At t, S believed of her A-ing that she would or might thereby V and
        (ii) At t, in what S knew that had not then slipped her mind, S had justification for this belief that was not, at the same time, justification for believing a proposition too far from the truth as to how she was actually going thereby to V», or
(3) It designates an aggregate of actions each of which was intentional and of each of which the following is true: «When S performed it, S believed of it and of the other component actions already performed or being performed that they would or might be parts of her V-ing».

At the moment, this definition seems to me to be satisfactory, so I offer it as the best answer I can now provide to the question of what makes an action intentional.

I do not want to leave the discussion of intentional action without saying something about a sort of case that I have not yet mentioned and that might be thought problematic, namely, the case of *absentminded* action. Consider, for example, someone who has recently changed residences but absentmindedly walks to her former residence at the end of the day, or someone who goes into his bedroom with the intention of changing clothes to go out for the evening, becomes absorbed in thinking about what makes an action intentional, and gets into his pajamas. There is certainly a temptation to say that these agents did not intend to be doing the things they did absentmindedly, and even that they did not do them intentionally. After all, when the agent "wakes up" to what she or he is doing, the agent will find it natural to say, "I did not mean to be doing this!".

I think, however, that it would be a mistake to deny either that such an absentminded action is intentional or that it is intended. What we should say about it, rather, is this: Although at the time she was doing it the agent intended to be doing it in the way she did it, and therefore did it intentionally, she had this intention only because she was at the time forgetting other intentions she had. The intention, like the action, was absentminded: It conflicted with those other intentions to which she was already committed and which she was not disposed to abandon; therefore, she would not have had this intention had the others not slipped her mind. When the absentminded person "wakes up" and says, "I did not intend to be doing this!", she is not really denying the intention to be doing this. Rather, she has to be taken to mean that she intended to be doing something incompatible with this: It is analogous to saying "I don't think so" when one means "I think not so".

This way of looking at absentminded actions – as genuinely intended and intentional – becomes compelling when one considers how much deliberation and problem solving can go into absentminded actions. They don't have to be automatic, zombielike, or even habitual. For example, suppose that it is Saturday morning and I deliberate about what to do that day, plan an excursion, figure out what route to take, what to take along, and so forth, and then carry out my plan. Clearly, there are many intended and intentional actions involved here. But they are all absentminded, for I have completely forgotten my intention to go to the wedding of a good friend that day. There is no reason to suppose that more habitual or automatic, absentminded actions differ from these deliberated ones with respect to the question of whether they are intended or intentional. They are all cases of a person's temporarily having an incoherent set of intentions; this is made possible by the person's failure actively to recall some of her intentions in a timely fashion. It is this incoherence in her mental state that makes the absentminded agent feel embarrassed and disturbed when she realizes what she is doing. It is not the feeling that she has temporarily lost intentional control of herself.

5

Free will versus determinism

Is freedom of the will compatible with determinism? I think not, and I would like to explain why.

First, let me explain what I take this venerable question to mean. By freedom of the will is meant *freedom of action*. I have freedom of action at a given moment if more than one alternative action is then *open to me*. Two or more actions are *alternatives* if it is logically impossible for me to do more than one of them at the same time. Two or more alternatives are *open to me* at a given moment if which of them I do next is entirely up to my choice at that moment: Nothing that exists up to that moment stands in the way of my doing next any one of the alternatives.

We all continually have the *impression* that our wills are thus free. For example, at most moments while I am sitting and talking or listening to someone, I have the impression that there are several alternative things I could do next with my right hand: gesture with it, scratch my head with it, put it on my lap, put it in my pocket, and so on. For each of these alternatives, it seems to me that nothing at all up to that moment stands in the way of my making it the next thing I do with my right hand; it seems to me that what has happened hitherto, the situation at that moment, leaves each of those alternatives still open to me to perform. And while I am conscious, I have similar impressions of open alternatives almost continually, not only about what I could do with my right hand but also, of course, about what I could do with my head, with my speech apparatus, and with my legs and feet. My impression at each moment is that *I at the moment,* and nothing prior to that moment, determine which of several open alternatives is the next sort of bodily exertion I voluntarily make.

90

It is impossible to imagine what one's conscious experience would be like were such an impression not a more or less continual feature of it. Perhaps any experience in which it seems to the subject that she wills or acts must include this impression of open alternatives, this impression of freedom.[1] Certainly it is an essential ingredient in any experience of consciously *deciding* which of several actions to do next, of making up one's mind whether to do this or that. I can now engage in deciding whether to turn right or left only if I have the impression that both alternatives are still open to me, that nothing now prevents my doing either one. If I believe that it is now too late for me to get on the next plane to London, then I cannot now engage in *deciding* whether or not to get on that plane. Knowing as I do that I cannot leap four feet straight up into the air (the condition of my legs prevents it), I cannot decide whether or not to do so: Nothing I might do now would count as my seriously deciding *not* to leap four feet straight up into the air; I could at best pretend to decide not to do that. So, inasmuch as I am frequently deciding what to do next, I frequently assume that I have alternatives open to me as to what I will do next.

But the fact that my making decisions commits me to the assumption that I have freedom does not establish that I do have freedom. It is, after all, possible to be quite mistaken in assuming that a certain alternative is open to one. I decide not to turn on the light, assuming that it is open to me to turn it on, but in fact the bulb is burned out. Nor does the fact that we cannot help continually having an impression of freedom of bodily action establish that we in fact ever do have such freedom. Even an inescapable impression can be an illusion. Witness our impression that the earth on which we stand is fixed and the sun and moon move around us daily. The most that might be established by the *inescapability* of the assumption or the impression of freedom is that we are justified in believing that we have freedom: How can we be reproached for this belief if we cannot help having it?

---

1 Searle (1984, p. 98) asserts that "evolution has given us a form of experience of voluntary action where the experience of freedom, that is to say, the experience of the sense of alternative possibilities, is built into the very structure of conscious, voluntary, intentional human behaviour".

Indeed, we need not be at all uneasy with our impression of freedom, as long as we have no specific reason to think that it might be illusory. But almost from the beginning of philosophy, people have, for one reason or another, doubted or denied that our wills are ever free. One reason is a certain thesis about the laws of nature called *determinism*. How much of what happens in the world do the laws of nature determine? Determinism says that they determine everything. More precisely, determinism says that, given the state of the world at any particular time, the laws of nature determine all future developments in the world, down to the last detail. Another convenient way of putting the thesis is this:

> A complete description of the state of the world at any given time and a complete statement of the laws of nature together entail every truth as to what events happen after that time.

For our purposes, we can take the determinism we are talking about to be what some philosophers have called *physical determinism* and have distinguished from what they call *psychological determinism*. An explicit formulation of physical determinism can be obtained by inserting the word *physical* before the words *state, nature,* and *events* in the preceding formulation:

> A complete description of the *physical* state of the world at any given time and a complete statement of the *physical* laws of nature together entail every truth as to what *physical* events happen after that time.

Physical determinism is a threat to free will if any determinism is. For if all physical events are determined in advance, then so also are all of our voluntary bodily exertions; and if volitions are naturally tied to brain events, as a good deal of evidence seems to indicate, then all of our volitions are also determined in advance if all physical events are so determined. We can say this without committing ourselves on the question of whether or not all mental states and processes are identical to or realized in physical processes. To say that volitions are naturally tied to neural processes is to say only that it is a law of nature that they be co-dependent: There can be a certain sort of volition on the part of a given agent if and only if there is a certain sort of physical process in his brain. This leaves open the question of whether or not the correlation is due to the identity of the realizations of the two sorts of processes.

Of course, if physical determinism is true, then an important part of traditional Cartesian dualism is false. For physical determinism entails that it can never be that what the body does depends essentially on antecedent events of a nonphysical sort, so that a difference in them, without any difference in antecedent physical events, would make a difference in what the body does. And this is contrary to what Descartes thought. On his view, the nonphysical mind has an autonomous influence on the body. (Note that Descartes's view does not entail that the workings of the mind are ever indeterministic, are not fully governed by psychological and psychophysical laws.)

Is determinism true? I don't know. And from what I hear, nobody else knows either. I am told that the preponderance of well-informed opinion is that quantum theory – the best theory physics has about electromagnetic phenomena and one whose predictive adequacy to the data of observation and experiment is extremely good – can explain certain observed results (for example, the Bell inequalities) only on the assumption that determinism is false. Still, even if most physicists and philosophers of physics nowadays are convinced that quantum theory must be right and determinism must be false, I am not sure that it would be true to say that anyone *knows* that determinism is false.

THE INTEREST OF THE QUESTION

If determinism is not known to be false, then that gives a very keen interest indeed to the question of whether or not free will is compatible with determinism. For if they are not compatible, and if we do not know determinism to be false, then we do not know whether or not we ever have freedom of action, whether or not we ever have alternative actions open to us. That is a disconcerting result, because we all have the impression and the belief in practice that we continually have freedom of action, and it is hard to see what it would be like for us not to have this impression and belief.[2]

2 Until about twenty years ago, it would have been taken for granted that another important issue that depends on whether freedom of action is compatible with determinism is whether *moral responsibility* is compatible with determinism. But Frankfurt (1969) offered examples that have persuaded many philosophers that it is possible for an agent to have been morally responsible for an action when no alternative action was open to her. More recently, Fischer (1982) has argued that, although Frankfurt's examples do not show that moral responsibility is compatible

As a matter of fact, we are not really better off even if we know determinism to be false in the ways that quantum theory says it is. For if determinism is incompatible with free will, so that a free action cannot be determined by the past state of the world and the laws of nature, then we have the freedom of will we like to think we have only if determinism is false in certain specific ways, only if the laws of nature and the antecedent states of the world leave open all or most of the alternative actions we like to think are open to us. But that determinism is false in all those specific ways does not follow from indeterministic quantum theory. So even if we know that indeterministic quantum theory is true, we cannot know by deduction therefrom that determinism has all the right exceptions. And it is clear that we do not know this in any other way either. In fact, we do not know enough about how the brain functions with respect to choice and volition to know even what the right exceptions would be. We do not know at just what locations in the brain we would need to find indeterministic processes or just what sorts of indeterministic processes allowed by physics would do the trick. It is, of course, possible to *speculate* about how determinism could be false in the right ways. This comes to speculation about the sorts of microevents in our brains that volitions (and other simple mental acts) depend on (or are realized in) and how these microevents in the brain might be undetermined in ways that quantum theory allows and that leave open the alternative volitions we typically think are open to us.[3]

Let us return to the main business: the question of the compatibility of freedom of action with determinism. I want first to develop an argument for their incompatibility, the best argument I can, and then to consider some objections to the argument.[4]

with determinism, they do show that having no alternative open to one is compatible with being "uncompelled [and even undetermined] in the actual sequence of events" and hence with being free in a sense (though not in the sense I have stipulated). I doubt both Frankfurt's and Fischer's claims, but I will not here undertake to examine them or the arguments offered for them. Whether they are true or not does not affect the reasons I offer in this section for the interest and importance of the question of whether determinism is compatible with having alternatives open to one. And to those reasons can be added this one: If determinism is, as I argue, *not* compatible with having alternatives open, then the question of whether Frankfurt's or Fischer's claims are true becomes all the more important.

3 There is some interesting speculation along these lines in Thorp (1980, pp. 67–71), some of which he derives from Eccles (1953, pp. 228ff) and Eccles (1970, p. 125).

4 The argument I will present is a descendant of one I presented in Ginet (1966),

Before laying out the argument, I want to comment on, and in some cases explain, some of the important notions it will use. First, regarding the notion of an action's being open to an agent, note that a proposition asserting that it was open to an agent to perform a certain action must contain, at least implicitly, two distinct temporal references, one for the time of the action and one for the time at which it was (still) open to the agent to perform it (at its time). In any intelligible proposition of this sort, either these times will be the same or the time at which the action was still open to the agent will be earlier than the time of the action. If an agent has a certain action at a certain time open to her at a given time, then she must have had it open to her at all earlier times, but she need not necessarily have it open to her at any later time. That is, from a proposition of the form «At t_2 it was open to S to do A at t_4», where t_2 is earlier than t_4, it follows that

(1) for any time t_1 earlier than t_2, it was at t_1 open to S to do A at t_4;

but it does *not* follow that

(2) for any time t_3 between t_2 and t_4, it was at t_3 open to S to do A at t_4.

(1) follows because, if there is an answer to the question of how, given her situation at t_2, S could have done A at t_4, then there is an obvious answer to the question of how, given her situation at t_1, S could have done A at t_4: namely, S could have done whatever she in fact did that allowed the situation to develop as it did until t_2, and then done whatever the answer to the first question prescribes. That (2) does *not* follow is clear from an example. I was in my house all morning. At 10:00 a.m. it was open to me to open the door of my campus office at 11:00 a.m. But the distance between my house and my campus office is such that at 10:55 a.m. it was *not* open to me to open the door of my campus office at 11:00 a.m.

Unless I indicate otherwise, in propositions of the form «It was

---

which had other, somewhat closer descendants in Ginet (1980) and Ginet (1983). It resembles the arguments for incompatibilism presented by van Inwagen (1974, 1975, 1983). It would perhaps be apt to think of all these not as different arguments, but as different versions of *the* argument for incompatibilism. The essential idea in all of them is the same: that it is never open to anyone to make the case negations of laws of nature or of truths entirely about the past. But the details in the formulations of specific versions are important: One version may contain error or be vulnerable to an objection where another version is not.

open to S to do A at t», I will take the implicit time of S's having the action open to her to be any time up to t. And in propositions of the form «At t it was open to S to do A», I will take the implicit time of the action to be t.

Next, I want to point out that we can distinguish between a broader and a narrower version of the notion of having an action open to one and to indicate that we will be using the broader notion. The distinction I have in mind depends on whether or not an agent's needing a significant amount of *luck* in order to perform a certain action is taken to rule that action out of those open to an agent. Suppose that I am a very inexpert dart thrower, but I happen by sheer luck to throw the dart into the bulls-eye. Or suppose that I do not know the combination for a lock I wish to open, but I happen by sheer luck to dial the right combination on my third try. One can have conflicting intuitions about such cases. On the one hand, it is natural to say that, since my action of hitting the bulls-eye with the dart (or of opening the lock) actually occurred, it must have been open to me to perform it. Even in the (far likelier) case where I fail to hit the bulls-eye (fail to dial the combination that opens the lock), we might accept the statement that with enough luck I could have hit it (could have opened it). On the other hand, it also seems natural to say that, since I had no skill at throwing darts (had no idea what the combination of the lock was) and it was sheer luck that I hit the bulls-eye (dialed the right combination), it was not open to me to do it, not something that I could do.[5]

This conflict of intuitions represents indecision as to what the requirements of the concept in question should be, so I think it is appropriate to say that each of two different concepts may be aptly expressed by the locution "It was open to S at t to perform action A". Hereafter I will use this locution to express the *weaker* or *broader* concept, that is, the one that does *not* make it a requirement that the action not have been performed by sheer luck, does *not* make it a requirement that the agent had the requisite knowledge or skill to

5 See the examples given by Dennett (1984, pp. 116–17) of the prisoner in a cell who does not realize that the cell door is unlocked and of the person who passes by a trashcan ignorant of the fact that it contains a purse full of diamonds. Here we may have conflicting intuitions as to whether it was open to the prisoner to leave the cell or open to the trashcan passer-by to acquire the purse full of diamonds. Dennett calls these *bare opportunities* and points out that when we want opportunities we want more than merely bare opportunities.

ensure her performance of it (or at least make it highly likely, rather than highly chancy, that she would perform it if she tried to do so).

We can define this broader notion in terms of the narrower one that does rule out luck:

> At t it was open to S (broad sense) to perform action A
> if and only if
> at t it was open to S (narrow sense) to perform some action such that, if S were to choose to perform that action, then S would perform action A (and it is not ruled out, nor is it required, that if S were to perform the action whereby S would perform A, S's performing A would be by luck rather than through skill or knowledge).

We can also define the narrower notion in terms of the broader one:

> At t it was open to S (narrow sense) to perform action A
> if and only if
> at t it was open to S (broad sense) to perform action A and, if S had tried to perform action A, S would not have needed great luck in order to do so (S had the skill or knowledge needed to make it highly likely that S would have performed action A had S tried to do so).

On these definitions, the narrow sense entails the broad sense: The set of actions narrowly open to an agent is a subset of those broadly open to her, satisfying a further special condition. Thus, if an agent does not have a given action broadly open to her, then she does not have it narrowly open to her. The incompatibilism for which I shall argue is the thesis that if determinism is true, then at no time does anyone have broadly open to her more than one alternative action. This entails the other incompatibilism, where *broadly* is changed to *narrowly*.[6]

I won't try now to explicate further either notion of having an action open to one. My argument for incompatibilism will not need an informative definition of these notions. What I have said is enough to identify them so that you know which intuitive notions in your repertoire to bring into play in understanding the argument. I suspect that the best strategy for defining them both ultimately in other terms would be to define the broad sense in other terms and then give the preceding definition of the narrow sense in terms of the broad one. I suspect also that one cannot give an interesting,

---

6 Van Inwagen (1983, pp. 230–1) has pointed out that a weak, luck-dependent sense of *can* is all that the argument for incompatibilism requires.

noncircular definition of either sense that avoids taking a position on the question of the compatibility of free will with determinism. An interesting, noncircular definition must be either compatibilist or incompatibilist; it cannot be neutral on this issue.

HAVING IT OPEN TO ONE
TO MAKE SOMETHING THE CASE

Another notion I need in formulating my argument for incompatibilism is less familiar than that of having an action open to one. It is the notion of having it open to one (at a given time) to make it the case that p, where p is some contingent proposition as to what occurs or obtains in the world at some particular time(s). This notion has having it open to one to perform a certain action (or actions) at a certain time (or times) as the special case where p attributes to one the action(s) in question. That is, "It is open to S at t to make it the case that she acts in such-and-such a way" means the same as "It is open to S at t to act in such-and-such a way". Understanding what is expressed by "It was open to S to make it the case that p" obviously requires understanding also the embedded notion of an agent's making it the case that p. Neither notion is in common parlance. They are equivalent to ordinary notions only in the special case where p attributes an action to S. In all other cases, they are philosophers' notions. But they are, or can be made, clear enough, and I find them indispensable in giving a fully explicit and precise formulation of the argument for incompatibilism.

Let me first say what I mean by sentences of the form «S made it the case that p». Though "made it the case that" is not an ordinary locution, it is a construction for which some rules of application that might be proposed will seem natural and appropriate and others will not. It is a construction out of familiar words that generates intuitions about what it would be appropriate for it to mean. The meaning that seems natural (to me, at any rate) is the following:

(a) S made it the case that p
    if and only if
    p and S caused (at least) the last thing needed for it to be the case that p.
(b) S caused (at least) the last thing needed for it to be the case that p
    if and only if
    an action of S's was or caused an event or state of affairs E such that E belongs to a set of events or states of affairs that was minimally sufficient

for the truth of p and that contains no event or state of affairs ending later than E did.

(c) A set of events or state of affairs was minimally sufficient for the truth of p

   if and only if

   the proposition that that set of events or states of affairs occurred – call this proposition q – entails p and any proposition entailing p that is weaker than q (that is, is entailed by but does not entail q) is equivalent to some proposition of the form «q or r».[7]

(I here take for granted the notions of an event and a state of affairs, and of an event's causing an event or a state of affairs. These are not everyday notions either, and it is notoriously difficult to give satisfactory noncircular definitions of them. But I think we have an intuitive grasp of them that is adequate for my purposes.)

A few minor points about this definition should be noted. First, it follows from it that if S caused an event E, then S made it the case that E occurred (for then the set containing just the event E will be a set minimally sufficient for the truth of the proposition that E occurred). This is so even if some event that S did not cause and that was later than S's action by which S caused E was causally necessary in the circumstances for the occurrence of E. For example, by placing in the luggage compartment of an airliner a bomb rigged to explode when its surrounding temperature went below a certain point, S caused the destruction of the airliner (and thus made it the case that the airliner was destroyed), even though S did not cause the critical event of the bomb's surrounding temperature going below a certain point.

Second, given this definition and my definition of an action in Chapter 1, any canonical personal event-designator of the form «S's making it the case that p at t» will designate an action. For of S's action that satisfies the definiens of (b), it will be true to say that S made it the case that p by that action; so the designator of that action has the GEN relation to «S's making it the case that p at t». Therefore, if the whole definition is to be informative, it is necessary to understand "an action of S's" in the definiens of (b) to mean an action that can be picked out by a designator in which the main gerund is *not* "making it the case" or any synonymous expression

---

7 It would not do to require merely that there is no proposition weaker than q that entails p, for this would not allow for the possibility that there is some condition other than q that is minimally sufficient for p.

(or that could be picked out without making use of "making it the case" or any synonymous expression).

Third, note that our definition allows for the possibility that the truth of p was overdetermined in such a way that S's contribution was not necessary (that is, it was false that had it not occurred, then it would not have been the case that p). For, besides the minimally sufficient condition that includes S's contribution, there could be another minimally sufficient condition that does not include it.

S made it the case that p if and only if S contributed the last thing needed to make up a minimally sufficient condition for the truth of p. This seems an appropriate definition in light of facts like the following. If R wrote a confidential memorandum on topic X and S gave a copy of it to the *New York Times,* then S made it the case that R's confidential memorandum on topic X was leaked, even though that proposition entails earlier events that S in no way contributed to bringing about, such as R's writing a confidential memorandum on topic X.[8] If our team scored four runs in the game and the only run I scored was the last one, then it seems perfectly natural to say that I, by scoring that run, made it the case that our team scored four runs in the game. If your only run was the second of our four, then it does *not* seem natural to say that you, by scoring your run, made it the case that we scored four runs in the game – despite the fact that your run was every bit as important a contribution to the total as mine. You brought the blackboard in here, and then I wrote on it the word *incompatibilism*. It seems appropriate to say that I, by writing *incompatibilism* on that board, made it the case that there was a board in here with the word *incompatibilism* on it. But it does not seem appropriate to say that you, by bringing the black-board in here, made it the case that there was a blackboard in here with the word *incompatibilism* on it – despite the importance of your contribution to bringing about that state of affairs.

Besides yielding such results for the case where p is a particular or existential proposition, our definition yields plausible results for the case where p is a universal generalization or the negation of a universal generalization. S made it the case that a given universal

---

8 If someone else gave a copy to the *Washington Post,* then that person too made it the case that R's memorandum was leaked. Between them, S and that person overdetermined the truth of that proposition.

generalization is true if and only if the generalization is true and S's action was or caused the last thing needed for the occurrence of the last confirming instance of the generalization. S made it the case that a given universal generalization is false if and only if it is false and S's action was or caused the last thing needed for the occurrence of some exception to the generalization (whether or not it is the last exception).

If that is what we mean by «S made it the case that p», what are the truth conditions for «It was open to S at t to make it the case that p»? One sufficient condition is obvious: This proposition will be true if in fact S did make it the case that p. (Remember, we are using the broad sense of «open to S».) But of course, that is not a necessary condition. If freedom of action is to be so much as logically possible, the truth of «It was open to S at t to make it the case that p» must be compatible with the falsity of «S made it the case that p».

Another obvious sufficient condition, one that I mentioned earlier, is obtained if p is a proposition attributing an action to S and it was open to S at t to perform that action. But there should be truth conditions for a much broader range of instantiations for p than that. In fact, whenever «S made it the case that p» expresses a true or a false proposition, so should «It was open to S at t to make it the case that p».

At this point, I will not attempt to work out any very informative condition that is both necessary and sufficient. I will state a rather uninformative one and then just put forward a few plausible assumptions about the truth conditions for «It was open to S at t to make it the case that p», assumptions on which the argument for incompatibilism will rely.

It will be convenient to have some abbreviatory notation:

$O_{st}p = def$ It was open to S at t to make it the case that p.

We can think of «O_{st}» as expressing a kind of operator on propositions. We can call it the *open possibility* operator and say that «$O_{st}p$» expresses the open possibility of proposition p relative to an agent S and a time t. This terminology should not, however, be taken to mean that the open-possibility operator obeys all the same logical principles as the *logical*-possibility operator obeys. It is clear that it does not. For instance: From the truth of p follows the logical possibility of p, but not its open possibility. For example, let p be the following: The earth continued in its orbit around the sun last year. From that truth does not follow the falsehood that it was at some time open to someone to make it the case that the earth continued in its orbit around the sun last year. «$O_{st}p$» could be read: «p was open-possible relative to S and t» but, of course, its meaning will be clearer in our original reading: «It was open to S at t to make it the case that p».

Now let us turn to the matter of the truth conditions for propositions of the form «$O_{st}p$». One thing is quite clear:

> It was open to S at t to make it the case that p
> if and only if
> it was open to S at t to act in such a way that had S so acted, S would thereby have made it the case that p.

This much is guaranteed simply by what we mean by «S made it the case that p», but this is not very informative. (We would have a truly informative account if we could provide a noncircular account of what it is for an agent to have an action open to her, a problem I will address later.) But from this general principle, certain useful subordinate principles do seem to follow.

First, it seems clear that if p is or is equivalent to a conjunction $(b_t \ \& \ a_t)$ where b_t is a *true* proposition entirely about what happened before t[9] and a_t is a proposition (true or false) as to what happens at or after t, then it was open to agent S at t to make it the case that p if it was open to S at t to make it the case that a_t. Given any truth entirely about the past, b_t, if I now have it open to me to make true a certain proposition about the future, a_t, then I now have it open to me to make true the conjunction of b_t and a_t. If I have it open to me now to make the world contain a certain event after now, then I have it open to me now to make the world contain everything that has happened before now plus that event after now.[10] We might call

---

9 I mean here that b_t reports what has been called a *hard fact* about the past before t. Intuitively, the idea is that everything needed to make b_t true was settled by t, that nothing that happened later had any bearing one way or the other on the truth of b_t. It seems a clear enough idea at the intuitive level. One has no great difficulty in applying it, in discriminating between truths that do express hard facts about the past and truths that do not. But to give the idea an informative, interesting analysis turns out to be a formidable task, as the recent literature on the problem attests. See, for example, Pike (1966), Saunders (1966), Adams (1967), Hoffman and Rosencrantz (1984), and Fischer (1983a, 1985, 1986b).

10 This principle expresses the same intuition that Nelson Pike expresses when he says:

this the principle that *freedom is freedom to add to the given past* or the principle of *the fixity of the given past*. We can express it in abbreviated notation as follows:

For all S, t, b_t, and a_t: if $O_{st}a_t$ then $O_{st}(b_t \ \& \ a_t)$.[11]

Here the variable a_t ranges over propositions as to what happens at or after time t and b_t ranges over *true* propositions as to what happens before t. The converse principle holds as well, but it will not be needed in the argument for incompatibilism.[12]

When assessing what is within my power at a given moment, I must take into account the way things are and the way things have been in the past. If we assume that what is within my power at a given moment determines a set of possible worlds, all of the members of that set will have to be worlds in which what has happened in the past relative to the given moment is precisely what has happened in the past relative to that moment in the actual world. (1977, p. 215)

When Pike speaks here of a set of possible worlds that is determined by what is in his power at a given moment, he does *not* mean the set of worlds in which it is true that he has in his power at that moment what he in fact has in his power then, as some commentators have unfortunately taken him to mean (see, for example, Hoffman, 1979). Of *that* set it would be wrong to say that all of its members have the same past as the actual world relative to the given moment. Rather, Pike means the smallest set of possible worlds that is such that, at the given moment, he has it in his power to make the actual world belong to that set. Of this set it is eminently plausible to assert that all its members have the same history up to that moment as the actual world. Suppose that it is now in my power to make it the case that *p*. Then it is now in my power to make the actual world contain the fact *p*. That is, it is in my power to make the actual world belong to the set of possible worlds that contain *p*. But it follows that there is a smaller set to which it is in my power to make the actual world belong, namely, the set of worlds that contain *p* and also have the same past as the actual world. It does not follow that it is in my power now to determine which unique total world containing *p* will be the actual one, for the future course of the world may depend on many other future events that are now undetermined and not in my power to determine. But if it is in my power to make the world contain *p*, then it follows that it is in my power to make the world contain everything that has happened up to now and *p*. This is just what the principle of the fixity of the given past says.
Van Inwagen (1983) expresses essentially this same intuition in his definition of "*s* can render *p* false" (p. 68):

It is within *s*'s power to arrange or modify the concrete objects that constitute his environment in some way such that it is not possible in the broadly logical sense that he arrange or modify those objects in that way and the past have been exactly as it in fact was and *p* be true.

11 In this and similar formulas throughout, "if . . . then . . ." expresses the material (truth-functional) conditional.
12 In earlier versions of the argument for incompatibilism (see Ginet, 1980, 1983),

103

This principle brings to light, by the way, another respect in which open possibility is not analogous to logical possibility. From the logical possibility of a conjunction follows the logical possibility of each conjunct. But from the open possibility relative to S and t of the conjunction $(b_t \;\&\; a_t)$ there does *not* follow the open possibility relative to S and t of b_t. This is evident from the fact that although something of the form $O_{st}(b_t \;\&\; a_t)$ can be true, no proposition of the form $O_{st}b_t$ can be true. Indeed, one of the principles that must hold in virtue of the truth conditions for propositions of the form $O_{st}p$

instead of the principle of the fixity of the given past I employed a stronger principle, which I called *modus ponens for power necessity*. This is formulated as follows: First, we define the *power necessity* operator, N_{st}:

$$N_{st}p =\mathrm{df}\; p \;\&\; \text{not-}O_{st}\text{not-}p.$$

Then *MP for power necessity* is the following principle:

If $N_{st}p \;\&\; N_{st}(\text{if } p \text{ then } q)$, then $N_{st}q$.

This principle is essentially the same as an inference rule that van Inwagen (1983) endorses in his version of the argument for incompatibilism (see his formulation of the rule [β], pp. 93–4).

David Widerker has pointed out to me that this principle is stronger than the argument needs. He has also persuaded me that it is too strong to be true by offering the following counterexample to it: Suppose that a bit of radium emitted a particle in room A at t_2, but its doing so was not determined by the laws of nature and the antecedent state of the world. At an earlier time t_1, it was open to Sam to move the bit of radium from room A to room B and keep it there until t_2, but he did not do so. This is surely a coherent story. Given it, if we let

p = it is not the case that the radium emitted a particle in room B at t_2,
q = it is not the case that between t_1 and t_2 Sam moved the radium from room A to room B and kept it there until t_2,
s = Sam, and
$t = t_1$,

we seem to have a counterexample to the principle of modus ponens for power necessity. The falsity of this instantiation of the principle's consequent, $N_{st}q$, is stipulated in the story: It was open to Sam at t_1 to make q false. And the story appears to make the instantiations of both conjuncts of the principle's antecedent true.

At first blush, one might think that the first conjunct, $N_{st}p$, is false in the story, that it *was* open to Sam at t_1 to make it the case that the radium emitted a particle in room B at t_2 by moving the radium to room B (doing that much *was* open to him); but this is to overlook the fact that, though the radium did emit a particle at t_2, it was not open to Sam to *make* the radium emit a particle at t_2 (or any other precise time). It is for a similar reason that the second conjunct, $N_{st}(\text{if } p \text{ then } q)$, is true. For this to be false, it would have to be open to Sam at t_1 to make it the case that $p \;\&\; \text{not-}q$. Now it was open to Sam to make q false but, had he done so, it would not have been open to him to make p true; for then that would require that it would have been open to him to make the radium *not* emit a particle at t_2, and that, of course, could no more have been open to him than to make it emit a particle at that precise time. See Widerker (1987).

104

is the following (where b_t, as before, ranges over true propositions as to what happened before t):

For all S, t, and b_t: not-$O_{st}b_t$ & not-O_{st}not-b_t.

That this holds is clear from our definition of «S made it the case that p» and the fact that, whatever actions S performs at t or thereafter, none will be or cause an event that occurred entirely before t. So there is no action open to S by performing which S would make it the case that b_t and also, of course, none by performing which S would make it the case that not-b_t. (If b_t is entirely about the past relative to t, then so is not-b_t.) To think otherwise would be to think that one could have it open to one to perform an action that, if performed, would cause an event prior to the action. It is a widespread and strong intuition that such backward causation is in principle impossible, that if there is any sense in which the past as such is now settled, it is that nothing that happens in the future can causally determine what happened in the past.

Second, it should surely be a fact about the truth conditions for «$O_{st}p$» that if p is deducible from the laws of nature, then it is never open to anyone to make it the case that not-p. If anything sets limits to what is open to natural agents, the laws of nature do. Indeed, this is part of the notion of a law of nature, part of what distinguishes such a law from a universal generalization that is only accidentally true (such as "All people named Carl Allen Ginet have no siblings").[13] Call this the principle of *the inescapability of the laws*. Adopting «Lp» as an abbreviation for «p is entailed by the laws of nature», we may express this principle in abbreviated notation as follows:

Lp only if for all s and t: not-O_{st}not-p.[14]

13 Suppose that one *defined* a notion for which this is true. One stipulates that by a *law* of nature* one means a law of nature (in the sense in which that expression is commonly used) that is such that no one ever has it open to her to make it the case that an exception to it occurs. Even if it were conceded that this is not a redundant definition, that it is not a *conceptual* truth that all laws of nature are laws* of nature, it would not follow that it is not a truth, much less that it is known to be false. Is it known to be false? How?
Suppose that one defined still another notion: By a *law** of nature* is meant any true universal generalization such that no one ever has it open to her make it the case that an exception to it occurs. Now substitute this notion for that of a law of nature in the definition of determinism and call the hypothesis thereby defined *determinism***. Is it known that determinism** is false? How?

14 In this and similar formulas throughout, *only if* expresses the material (truth-functional) conditional, with the left component being the antecedent and the right component being the consequent.

The argument derives in a straightforward way from our two principles. Determinism entails that, for any truth a as to what will be the case, there is a truth b entirely about the past such that it follows from the laws of nature that if b then a; thus, by the inescapability of the laws, it follows that it was never open to anyone to make it the case that b & not-a; from this last plus the principle of the fixity of the given past, it follows that it was never open to anyone to make it the case that not-a. Stipulating that the variable b_t ranges over *truths* entirely about what happened before t and the variable a_t ranges over *truths* about what happens at or after t, and using the abbreviations previously introduced, we can present the argument more formally as follows. Determinism entails:

1. For any t and a_t there is a b_t: $L(\text{if } b_t \text{ then } a_t)$.
2. For any t and a_t there is a b_t: $L\text{not-}(b_t \& \text{not-}a_t)$.   1
3. For any s, t, and a_t there is a b_t: $\text{not-}O_{st}(b_t \& \text{not-}a_t)$.
                             2, inescapability of the laws
4. For any s, t, and a_t there is a b_t: if $O_{st}\text{not-}a_t$ then $O_{st}(b_t \& \text{not-}a_t)$.
                             fixity of the given past
5. For all s, t, and a_t: $\text{not-}O_{st}\text{not-}a_t$ 3, 4

Two things about this argument are clear and beyond dispute: First, the argument shows that if our two principles about open possibility are correct, then determinism entails the conclusion of the argument, proposition 5; second, if determinism entails proposition 5, then incompatibilism holds: for proposition 5 says that for any time t and any fact as to what happens at t or thereafter, that fact was unavoidable at t by any agent. Thus, if determinism is true, no agent ever has it open to her to make the case any propositions as to what happens in the world other than those propositions that are actually true; in any possible world where determinism is true, it is never the case that any agent has it open to her to determine which of several alternative (contrary) propositions will be the case. It follows that if determinism is true, no agent ever has more than one alternative action open to her and, therefore, that free will (as I've defined it) does not exist. This follows because, by our definition of what it is to make something the case, an agent has it open to her to make something the case if and only if she has it open to her to perform some action whereby she would make that thing the case.

Thus anyone who wishes to reject the conclusion that determinism entails the nonexistence of free will must deny at least one of our two principles. Which of these such a thinker will be bold enough to deny will depend, I think, on which of two competing views she holds regarding the truth conditions for certain relevant counterfactual conditionals.[15]

The two views on counterfactuals are the *backtracking* view and the *Local Miracle* view. The issue between the two views is this: Suppose that an event has occurred that is determined by the laws of nature and the states of the world at prior times. Call this event E. Now suppose that we consider the contrary-to-fact situation in which E did not occur; we say, "If E had not occurred, then . . ." Are we then considering a situation, a world, in which the laws of nature are all the same as in the actual world, but the states of the world prior to E are different in ways they would have to be in order to permit E's nonoccurrence compatibly with the same laws? Or are we considering a world in which the past is the same as in the actual world, but E's occurrence is permitted by a small local exception to the laws of nature (whatever exception makes the laws of this other world depart from those of the actual world in as small and local a way as possible)?

David Lewis takes the latter view (except for certain very special cases) on the grounds that the latter world (in which the laws are somewhat different) more closely resembles the actual world than does the former world (in which the past is vastly different). And that seems to me the better view to take.

But if one does take the other, backtracking view[16] *and* one still resists incompatibilism, despite our argument for it, then one will be forced, I think, to deny the principle that if it is now open to one to make the world contain a certain event, then it is now open to one to make it contain that event *and* everything that happened up to now. This backtracking compatibilist will have to think in the following way:

---

15 In what I have to say about this, I am indebted to Fischer (1983b), Fischer (1988), and Fischer ed. (1986b, pp. 32–40). With respect to the objection to the inescapability of the laws, I am indebted also to Lewis (1981).

16 As does, for example, Bennett (1984, pp. 57–91).

Since incompatibilism is false, there is some condition that is both compatible with determinism and such that I must regard it as sufficient for the truth of $O_{st}a_t$ for some false proposition a_t. Call such a compatibilist-sufficient condition, whatever it might be, $C_{st}a_t$. (Any plausible candidate for $C_{st}a_t$ will be a condition on the causal history of S's doing whatever action or inaction S was actually engaged in instead of doing what, had she done it, would have made it the case that a_t, and it will be a condition that obtains in actual cases of normal actions that, apart from worries about determinism, seem to be ones that the agents could have avoided, ones for which there were alternatives open to the agents.) Suppose that determinism is true and for some false proposition, a_t, $C_{st}a_t$ is true and therefore, on my view, $O_{st}a_t$ is true. For example, a_t is the proposition that S scratches the back of her head within one minute after t. Since determinism is true, there is a true proposition b_t such that L (b_t only if not-a_t). If we ask, "What if S had made it the case that a_t?", then on my backtracking view, the true counterfactual answer here is

(BT)   If it had been the case that a_t, then it would have been the case that not-b_t.

From (BT) it follows that it was *not* open to S to make it the case that (b_t & a_t). And this, conjoined with $O_{st}a_t$, contradicts the principle of the fixity of the given past.

At this point, the backtracking compatibilist must face the following question: If the principle of the fixity of the given past is false, how is it that we seem so strongly inclined to make inferences in accord with it? For instance, given the premises that I have done twenty push-ups in the last five minutes and that it is now open to me to do four push-ups in the next minute, we would find it natural to conclude therefrom that it is now open to me to make it the case that by the end of the next minute I will have done twenty-four push-ups in six minutes (the twenty I did in the last five minutes plus four more in the next minute). Such inferences are quite common and quite compelling. It cannot be that we are always in error in making them.

The only plausible strategy for the backtracking compatibilist in response to this challenge is to hold that we are comporting ourselves properly in such inferential episodes because there is more to them than meets the eye. In them we do not really assume the truth of the principle in question because we always rely on an additional tacit premise, besides the if-clause of that principle. The principle, recall, is the following:

108

For all S, t, b_t, and a_t: if $O_{st}a_t$ then $O_{st}(b_t \ \& \ a_t)$.

In the inferences under consideration, says the backtracking compatibilist, we only seem to rely on this principle. In actuality, we rely on a principle that, although it has the same consequent as this one, conjoins with its antecedent something further (which we take for granted and do not bother to state). That is, we actually use a principle of the following form:

(Z)   For all S, t, b_t, and a_t: if $O_{st}a_t \ \& \ \boldsymbol{X}$ then $O_{st}(b_t \ \& \ a_t)$.

This response is not just a plausible strategy for the backtracking compatibilist; it is a position she must adopt. She must hold that when we make inferences that seem to be in accord with the principle of the fixity of the given past, we assume that, besides $O_{st}a_t$, the following backward-looking conditional is true:

(1) If it had been the case that a_t, then it would have been the case that b_t.

Otherwise, if the true conditional is this:

(2) If it had been the case that a_t, then it would have been the case that not-b_t

then it would not have been open to S at t to make it the case that $(b_t \ \& \ a_t)$.

But this is not a comfortable position for the backtracking compatibilist. For on the backtracking account of its truth conditions, conditional (1) will be far from obviously true in a great many cases where we are ready to infer confidently from $O_{st}a_t$ to $O_{st}(b_t \ \& \ a_t)$. Thus it is implausible to suggest that we confidently assume the truth of such a conditional in making such inferences.

For instance, suppose that S did twenty push-ups in the five minutes ending at t and then stopped doing push-ups for a while. Let a_t be the false proposition:

(a_t) S did four push-ups in the minute after t.

Let b_t be the true proposition:

(b_t) S did twenty push-ups in the five minutes before t.

When we know that (b_t) S did twenty push-ups in five minutes, we will confidently believe on that basis that, if $(O_{st}a_t)$ at t, S could have done four push-ups in the next minute after t, then at t, S could have made it the case that $(b_t \ \& \ a_t)$ she had done twenty-four push-ups in six minutes – seemingly subscribing to the principle of the fixity of the given past. The backtracking compatibilist must say that we feel entitled to this confident belief only because we feel entitled to assume (possibly among other things) that if S had done four push-ups in the minute after t, then it would still have been the case that S did twenty push-ups in the five minutes before t (so that it is not the fixity of the given past that we use in our reasoning here but something of the form of the substitute principle [Z], with X being or entailing conditional [1]).

But this that the backtracking compatibilist must say is highly implausible. For it is implausible to suppose that, in the common-place sort of case we are talking about, we would feel entitled to assume that the backtracking truth condition for that counterfactual conditional does obtain. For, in assuming this, we are assuming that in a *nearest* possible world where S did do four push-ups in the minute after t *and the laws of nature are exactly the same as in the actual world* (that is, a possible world meeting those conditions that is at least as similar to the actual world as any other meeting them), it would be true that S did twenty push-ups in the five minutes before t. Thus, it would not be enough to be sure that $(b_t$ & $a_t)$ is compatible with the laws of nature. One would also have to be sure that a world in which $(b_t$ & $a_t)$ and the same laws of nature hold is more similar to the actual world than any in which (not-b_t & $a_t)$ and the same laws of nature hold. And that is very hard to be sure of, since any minimal set of changes in the past needed to permit a_t to be true is likely to ramify vastly into the past (especially if determinism is true), and it may, for all we know, do so in such a way that the very different state of the world at some distant past time plus the same laws of nature would entail not-b_t.

Thus it appears that, though the backtracking compatibilist needs to explain away our seeming reliance on the principle of the fixity of the given past, needs to make it out that when we seem to use that principle what we really use is something of the form of (Z), she has no plausible way of doing this. Indeed, she is forced into a highly implausible explanation by the necessity of holding that the additional premise she claims we must assume, the X in (Z), entails that the backtracking truth condition for «if it had been that a_t, then it would (still) have been that b_t» obtains.

The compatibilist who holds the Local Miracle view of the truth conditions for counterfactual conditionals, on the other hand, can accept the fixity of the given past. For she can plausibly claim that the conditional «if it had been that a_t, then it would (still) have been that b_t» is, necessarily, always true when it is true that $O_{st}a_t$. For on the Local Miracle account of their truth conditions, such conditionals are trivially true.

(The Local Miracle view can allow for exceptions, cases where, for some false a_t and true b_t, if it had been that a_t, then it would have to have been that not-b_t. But then it must hold that in any such case, it must also be false that $O_{st}a_t$. This will be so if, as seems plausible, the required truth condition in any such case is that not-b_t was necessary in the circumstances for a_t. For example, if it is true that Jones was at the faculty meeting at ten minutes before noon and it is true that, if he had been in the airport at noon, then it would have to have been the case that he was not at the faculty meeting at ten minutes before noon, then it must also be true that it was not open to Jones at any time during that ten minutes to make it the case that he was in the airport at noon.)

And, we might note, even the backtracker, *if she is an incompatibilist*, can hold that the truth of «if it had been that a_t, then it would (still) have been that b_t» is necessary for the truth of «$O_{st}a_t$». For on the incompatibilist view, «$O_{st}a_t$» can be true only if it is not antecedently determined by the laws of nature that not-a_t; and that means that the backtracking truth condition for that conditional is satisfied: Those worlds in which a_t and the same laws of nature hold that are more similar to the actual world than any others will be exactly the same as the actual world up to t and will thus include b_t.

The compatibilist who takes the Local Miracle view about the truth conditions for counterfactual conditionals can, as we said, cheerfully accept the principle of the fixity of the given past. And she can say that the counterfactual that always holds in situations where not-a_t, b_t, and $O_{st}a_t$ hold is the following:

(LM)   If it had been that a_t, then it would (still) have been that b_t.

This compatibilist will, however, be obliged to deny the principle that it is not open to anyone to falsify the laws of nature.[17] For,

111

from (LM) and «$O_{st}a_t$», it follows that $O_{st}(b_t \& a_t)$, from which it follows that O_{st} not-(if b_t then not-a_t). From this last and the inescapability of the laws, it follows that not-L (if b_t then not-a_t). But the compatibilist holds that there are such situations (that is, ones where not-a_t, b_t, and $O_{st}a_t$ hold) in which it is true that L (if b_t then not-a_t). So, from compatibilism and the claim that (LM) holds in such situations, it follows that the principle of the inescapability of the laws is false.

A case *for* the inescapability of the laws is made by Peter van Inwagen,[18] who gives examples concerning which we feel powerfully inclined to reason in a way that assumes that this principle holds. Among his examples is this: If one acknowledges that it is a law of nature that nothing travels faster than the speed of light, then one must acknowledge that no one has it open to her to make it the case that protons travel faster than the speed of light; it would be incoherent to think that it follows from the laws of nature that no human being can be deprived of vitamin C without getting scurvy and at the same time think that one could bring it about that a human being is deprived of vitamin C without getting scurvy. David Lewis and John Fischer say that such examples do not support the inescapability of the laws, because the inference that they show us willing to make can be justified by a different and narrower principle, one that does not entail the inescapability of the laws.[19] The most that such examples show, they say, is that we find compelling this narrower principle; they do not show that our concept of a law of nature commits us to the inescapability of the laws.

The narrower principle that Lewis and Fischer adduce to explain such examples is the following:

(Y) Lp only if it is never open to anyone to perform an action that would be or cause an event that falsifies p.

(An event falsifies p if and only if, necessarily, if that event occurs, then p is false.) Recall the principle of the inescapability of the laws:

Lp only if for all s and t: not-O_{st} not-p.

(Y) is weaker than this principle, because the proposition on the right side of (Y) does not entail that it was never open to anyone

---

17 As Lewis (1981) has pointed out.
18 In van Inwagen (1983, pp. 61–2, 92, 1974, and 1975).
19 See Lewis (1981) and Fischer (1988).

to make it the case that not-p. For, on our account of "making it the case that", making it the case that not-p would not require performing an action that would be or cause an event that entails not-p. Therefore, it might never be open to anyone to perform any such action, but would still be open to someone at some time to make it the case that not-p. For example, let p be as follows:

(p)   It is not the case both that Jupiter existed two million years ago and that I drank coffee today.

I did make it the case that not-p (that is, that Jupiter existed two million years ago and I drank coffee today); hence I had it open to me to do so. But neither I nor anyone else performed any action that entails not-p or that caused an event that entails not-p (since not-p entails that Jupiter existed two million years ago) and no one ever had it open to her to perform such an action. So the consequent of (Y) is true for this p, but the consequent of the principle of the inescapability of the laws is false. (That was an example where p itself is false. For one where p is true, replace *coffee* with *slivovitz*.)

So in our supposed situation, it is compatible with (Y), but not with the inescapability of the laws, that it is open to S at t to make it the case that not-(b_t only if not-a_t) $[= (b_t$ & $a_t)]$ by making it the case that a_t, provided that the action by which S would be able to make it the case that a_t (or the action–result sequence by which S would be able to do so) would not in itself falsify (b_t only if a_t) (or any other proposition entailed by the laws of nature).

Lewis and Fischer say that it is (Y), and not the inescapability of the laws, that captures how we conceive a law of nature to limit our freedom, that expresses what we are really willing to deduce from «Lp». In van Inwagen's examples, what we feel compelled to deduce is only what (Y) tells us follows, namely, that no one can perform an action that would be or cause a proton's traveling faster than the speed of light, that no one can perform an action that would be or cause someone's being deprived of vitamin C without getting scurvy. There is no need for appeal to the inescapability of the laws rather than (Y) to justify the inferences we find compelling in those cases.

I think, however, that we can show that our conception of the limit placed on our freedom by the laws of nature is stronger than this. Here is an example where (Y) is *not* adequate to explain what we are willing to deduce. Suppose that some time before t, S in-

113

gested a drug that quickly causes a period of complete unconscious-
ness that lasts for several hours. Suppose that, because of the drug,
there is true of S a certain proposition of the form

At t, S's neural system was in state U

and it follows from this proposition and the laws of nature that S
was unconscious for at least thirty seconds after t. If we let

b_t = At t, S's neural system was in state U
a_t = Beginning at t plus five seconds, S voluntarily exerted
force with her right arm for ten seconds,

then our supposition about the laws of nature here is that L (b_t only
if not-a_t) [= Lnot-(b_t & a_t)]. If we know all this, then we are surely
entitled to deduce that it was not open to S to voluntarily exert force
with her arm in the five seconds after t, that is, not-$O_{st}a_t$.

But (Y) is not enough to justify this deduction. For S's voluntarily exerting force with her arm in that ten seconds, if it had
happened, would not itself have been or caused an event that contradicts the laws of nature. So we cannot reach the conclusion that it is
not open to S at t to make a_t the case by finding this to be a case of
its not being open to S to perform an action that would be or cause
an event that falsifies the laws. We must use a different basis.

It seems that the reasoning that justifies our conclusion must go
as follows: Since (b_t & a_t) [= (at t, S's neural system was in state U
and from t plus five to t plus fifteen seconds, S voluntarily exerted
force with her right arm)] contradicts the laws of nature, it was not
open to S at t to make that proposition the case (here an inference
in accordance with the inescapability of the laws); therefore, given
the truth of b_t, it was not open to S at t to make it the case that a_t
(by the principle of the fixity of the given past). The example seems
to show that we think of the laws of nature as limiting our freedom, not merely in the way expressed by (Y), but also in the way
expressed by the principle of the inescapability of the laws.

The compatibilist may reply that, although the example shows
that we rely on something stronger than (Y), its apparent dem-
onstration that we rely on the inescapability of the laws is still an
illusion. The compatibilist may support this claim by appealing to
popular compatibilist ideas about what sort of condition is sufficient
for an action to have been avoidable by its agent. Many compatibilists have said roughly the following: The proposition that S's
doing A at t_2 was at an earlier time, t_1, unavoidable by S is *not* en-

tailed merely by the proposition that S's doing A at t_2 was nomically necessitated by the state of the world at t_1. Rather, this is entailed only when that proposition is conjoined with the further proposition that causing S to do A at t_2 by that antecedent state of the world did *not* go through S's antecedent motivational states and processes (S's relevant beliefs, desires, intentions, etc.) in a certain way that is exemplified in normal, seemingly free actions (whatever way that is).[20] On the basis of that sort of idea, a compatibilist might offer the following attempt to explain away the appearance that my example supports the principle of the inescapability of the laws. We tend to read into the premise of our reasoning about such examples, that L (b_t only if not-a_t), more than it really says. We know from the description of the example that the nomic necessitation from b_t (at t, S's neural system was in state U) to not-a_t (it was not the case that at t plus five seconds S voluntarily exerted force with her arm for ten seconds) does *not* go through S's motivational history in the appropriate way, the way that, by compatibilist lights, would be sufficient for S to have it open to her at t to make it the case that a_t. In making the inference from «L (b_t only if not-a_t)» to «not-O_{st} not-(b_t only if not-a_t)» (and thence via the principle of the fixity of the given past to «not-$O_{st} a_t$»), we tend to add that information to the premise. That tacit supplementation of the premise is essential to our feeling entitled to draw the conclusion. So it is not really the principle of the inescapability of the laws that we rely on in the first step, but a principle that adds to its antecedent this tacit premise.

The only way to defend the inescapability of the laws against this attack is to deny the suggestion about the notion of unavoidability on which it is based (the suggestion that freedom to do otherwise is not lost if one's action is nomically necessitated by one's motives and will in an appropriate way). This suggestion seems less plausible when one thinks about what it would be like really to know the laws of nature governing the causing of particular actions by their agents' motives and to use this knowledge to manipulate agents. Suppose that we observe a man get out of his chair, go to the kitchen sink, and get a drink of water: an ordinary sequence

20 For a recent compatibilist suggestion of this sort, see Slote (1982). Some such idea seems to be behind the conditional analyses of freedom that compatibilists have traditionally offered: They try to capture the idea of the right sort of causal history of the action by a subjunctive conditional that indicates what difference in S's motivational history would have led to a different action.

of actions that appears to be freely undertaken at every step. But then we learn that this man's brain has been programmed and the environment arranged so that exactly those movements on his part would be causally necessitated by those antecedently arranged circumstances, and that all this was known in advance by those who did the arranging. They explain the relevant causal laws and show us how they can do the same thing with anybody. Our impression that here was an agent acting freely, with alternatives open to him, vanishes completely. And it would not be restored by our learning that during the episode the man had the normal impression of freedom, of having alternatives open to him, and his movements were the outcome of his perceptions and motives in the sort of way such things normally are. What we have learned would compel us to view him as *not* having it open to him (after the initial arrangements) to do other than what he did. And we would be compelled to this view via an inference of the form given in the principle of the inescapability of the laws (as part of a more complex inference of the form given in our argument for incompatibilism).

At this point, some compatibilists might be tempted to say that what makes my latest example a case of unavoidable action – what is *necessary* to make it such a case – is that the antecedent state of the world that causally necessitates the action, through the agent's motivational states and processes in a normal sort of way, did not itself come about in a normal sort of way. The fact that that antecedent state was arranged by other agents with the intention of manipulating this agent, rather than having come about naturally, is what makes this a case of an unavoidable action.[21]

All I can say about this suggestion is that it seems to me very implausible on its face. Why should the fact that manipulation-minded agents, rather than nature or blind chance, arranged the state of the world that causally necessitated this episode in this agent's life make any difference to the unavoidability of that episode by that agent? Suppose that we came to know of two cases – first, a case involving manipulators as described previously, and then later, another case where the very same sort of antecedent state of the world as the manipulators arranged in the first case happened to come about naturally – and we knew how such an antecedent state causally neces-

---

21 Some remarks in Dennett (1984) suggest this line of thought; see, for example, p. 8 on "The Nefarious Neurosurgeon".

sitates such an episode as was in fact experienced by both agents. Would we find it *any less* compelling to say of the second, naturally occurring case that such an episode was unavoidable by the agent after the time of the antecedent state than to say this of the first, artificially arranged case? No! As soon as we learn about the naturally occurring case that there was here the same antecedent state of the world that causally necessitated the episode in the artificially arranged case, our impression that here was an agent with alternatives open to him, with free will, will vanish completely. And it will not be restored by its being pointed out to us that here *blind nature,* rather than any agent, arranged the causally necessitating antecedent state.

APPROACHING AN INFORMATIVE ANALYSIS OF OPEN POSSIBILITY

Let me now say something about how an informative, noncircular analysis of open possibility might be arrived at. As we said earlier, it is obvious that

$O_{st}p$ (= It was open to S at t to make it the case that p)
if and only if
it was open to S at t to act in such a way that had S so acted, S would thereby have made it the case that p.

This analysis still employs the notion of open possibility, but applied only to the agent's own action. We can give a more informative, noncircular, necessary, and sufficient condition for O_{st}, one that does not use the notion of open possibility at all, if we can give one for S's having an action open to her.

We can do this if we can give one for S's having a *basic* action open to her. A basic action is one designated by a basic action-designator, a notion we defined in Chapter 1 ("The Definition of Action"). Every action is either basic or an action that the agent performs by performing some basic action (or it is an aggregate of actions of these types). So, for example, my turning on the light was *not* basic because it consisted in my moving the light switch in a certain way and that action's causing the light to go on: I turned on the light by moving the switch. And my moving the light switch was not basic either, because I did that by exerting force with my hand and fingers in a certain way, thereby causing the switch to move. Nor was my exerting force with my hand and fingers basic, for I did that by means of a mental activity of volition, of willing to exert with

117

my arm and hand in a certain way, which is a basic action. On my view, basic actions are all volitions or other sorts of causally simple mental acts. That is a controversial view, but that issue does not matter for the problem that presently engages us. Whatever basic actions are, the correct account of what it is for such an action to be open to an agent will be the same.

Let us introduce some abbreviations for notational convenience. Let us reserve A, with or without subscripts, for denoting basic action types. Let $A(s, t)$ stand for "S performed basic action A at t". Thus $O_{st} A(s, t)$ stands for "It was open to S at (that is, up to) t to perform basic action A at t".

Our question, then, is: Given an agent S, a time t, and a basic action type A, what will specify a necessary and sufficient condition for the truth of «$O_{st} A(s, t)$» without using open possibility as an undefined element in the specification? As I said earlier, what one thinks is an acceptable answer to this question will depend on whether one is a compatibilist or an incompatibilist. That is, part of the problem in deciding on the correct account is deciding that issue. It means deciding whether or not the following should be part of the desired specification:

(U)   For no b_i: $L(b_i$ only if not-$A(s, t))$

Incompatibilism holds that this is a necessary condition; compatibilism holds that it is not. For in the case where «$A(s, t)$» is false, «$O_{st} A(s, t)$» is incompatible with determinism (the thesis of incompatibilism) if and only if «$O_{st} A(s, t)$» entails that (U) holds. Compatibilist and incompatibilist must disagree on the necessity of that condition.

But even if that is a necessary condition, it is likely not the only one. It may, for example, be the case that some unavoidable actions done out of psychological compulsion are not nomically necessitated by antecedent conditions, that what is sufficient to establish compulsion by, say, a drug addict's craving or a terrified person's panic, is not sufficient to establish nomic necessitation by antecedents. Compatibilist and incompatibilist should be able to agree on what other conditions – ones not entailing (U) – are necessary. Whether or not a particular other condition is necessary cannot depend on the compatibilism – incompatibilism issue, since the only thing decided by one's position on that issue is whether or not (U) is necessary. Thus a cogent argument that another, independent condition is necessary will be cogent for compatibilist and incompatibilist alike. Therefore, the best possible compatibilist specification of a condition necessary and sufficient for the truth of «$O_{st} A\,(s,t)$» will be something that the incompatibilist can accept as necessary. For if the compatibilist does not have cogent reasons for regarding it as necessary, then she does not yet have the best possible compatibilist suggestion for a necessary and sufficient condition.

So the incompatibilist can say this: Take the most plausible suggestion of a condition necessary and sufficient for the truth of «$O_{st} A\,(s,t)$» that is possible for the compatibilist to make, that lacks nothing from the point of view of compatibilism, that would *be* necessary and sufficient if compatibilism were correct, and abbreviate it (whatever it is) by «$C_{st} A\,(s,t)$». Then this will be a correct account as far as it goes, a necessary condition, needing only to be conjoined with the condition given earlier to be wholly correct, a necessary and sufficient condition. So, once the compatibilist has done her work and given us the specification of «$C_{st} A\,(s,t)$», the task for the incompatibilist is easy. The incompatibilist just asserts:

$O_{st} A\,(s,t)$
if and only if
(U) for no b_t: L (if b_t then not-$A\,(s,t)$) & $C_{st} A\,(s,t)$.

Since I am persuaded by the argument for incompatibilism, this is the shape that I believe the account must take. And I just wish that the compatibilists would get on with their part of the job and give us an informative and clearly acceptable specification of the second conjunct.

The nonlazy incompatibilist has a motive for helping the compatibilist to devise the best possible compatibilist suggestion, because, when it is conjoined with (U), it will give the best *incompatibilist* account. Of course, approaching the other conjunct in the compatibilist way may result in its entailing something already entailed by (U), but there is no harm in such redundancy. The important thing is that this approach will not bring into the analysis anything that the incompatibilist cannot regard as necessary.

What is the best possible suggestion that the compatibilist can make? What should «$C_{st} A\,(st)$» abbreviate? I will attempt to give only a sketch of what the high-level shape of the answer to this question might be. I will not attempt to work out the details of the really informative account we all would like to have; that is too large and difficult a task to attempt here.

If we take «S's motives» to comprise all of S's psychological states that are apt to have an influence on S's basic actions – appetites, desires, emotions, beliefs, including moral and evaluative beliefs, and so on, whether standing or occurrent – then one thing we will want «$C_{st} A\ (st)$» to entail is

(N)   It is not the case that something outside S's motives nomically necessitated not-$A\ (s, t)$ via a process that did not go through S's motives.

(This is already entailed by (U), but we are not worrying about that, since we are looking for what the compatibilist as well as the incompatibilist must regard as necessary.)

But (N) does not seem enough. A compatibilist must recognize other ways, not ruled out by (N), in which an action or nonaction can be rendered unavoidable. If, for example, S's A-ing at t would be S's continuing to do something extremely painful and S has reached the point where he can bear no more pain, or if panic produced by the apprehension of some terrifying threat, or an irresistible craving induced by S's drug addiction compels S to do something contrary to A at t, then perhaps we have a situation in which it was not in S's power, and therefore not open to S, to A at t. But it is not a situation that is ruled out by (N), because the compulsion in all these examples arises from within S's motives (as we have broadly defined that term). So we need to add something like this:

(C)   It is not the case that something in S's motives irresistibly *compelled* S to something incompatible with S's A-ing at t.

Here is where my account gets sketchy indeed. We need an account of what it is to be irresistibly compelled by pain, emotion, appetite, desire, or the like. And that is not easy to give. The chief difficulty is how to draw the line (even a vague, fuzzy line) between what is genuinely irresistible and what is only very difficult to resist. Genuine psychological compulsion that renders the subject powerless to do otherwise must be distinguished from weakness of will where the subject could have resisted but did not try hard enough. Weakness of will is not having a will that is too weak, like having too little strength in one's muscles, but not exercising one's will to its maximum strength. Thus it would be a mistake to define a compulsive motive as one that is in conflict with that part of S's motives with which S identifies herself.[22] Such a motive need not be

---

22 According to Frankfurt (1971), these are S's higher-order volitions. According to Watson (1975), they are S's considered values.

genuinely compulsive. Nor need a genuinely compulsive motive be such an opposed-to-the-self motive. The *willing* addict may be compelled and have no alternative open to him as much as the unwilling one.[23] And even the agent who goes against his better judgment may not be the victim of a compulsive motive, but rather may be exhibiting weakness of will.

But what is the criterion of the difference? How it seems to the subject at the time is surely central to it. But this is a defeasible criterion. People can fool themselves. "Naturally, you *wanted to think* that you could resist no more, because it was so difficult or painful to do so." So perhaps a plausible criterion would be as follows: It seemed to the subject to be irresistible, and the subject was not deceiving herself about that. Even if this is right as far as it goes, it is not yet nearly as informative as we would like. We would like to have a better understanding of self-deception in these matters. But it is as far as I can go here.

So the two conditions I conjoin to make my sketch of a suggestion of a truth condition for «$C_{st} A (s, t)$», the best compatibilist condition for the open possibility of a basic action $A (s, t)$, are (N) and (C). $C_{st} A (s, t)$ if and only if (N) & (C). Since (N) is entailed by the incompatibilist necessary condition (U), my suggestion for an incompatibilist necessary and sufficient condition is the conjunction of (U) and (C):

$O_{st} A (s, t)$ if and only if
(U) for no b_i: $L (b_i$ only if not-$A (s, t))$ &
(C) it is not the case that something in S's motives irresistibly *compelled* S to something incompatible with S's A-ing at t.

Once we have a noncircular account of the open possibility of a basic action, we have done the hardest part of the task of giving a noncircular account of the open possibility of making something the case, but we have not quite completed it. How the former enters into the latter is more complex than we have so far noted.

It will not do to say simply the following:

$O_{st} p$ if and only if
there is a time t^*, not earlier than t, and a basic action type A such that

---

23 While not denying this, Frankfurt (1969, 1971) argues that, despite not having an alternative in his power, the willing addict, though not the unwilling one, is morally responsible for what his irresistible craving compels him to do.

(a) $O_{st} A (s, t^*)$ and
(b) if S had A-ed at t^*, then S would have made it the case that p.

It was open to me on Saturday to make it the case that I had ten pages of notes for my Monday lecture by Sunday evening but, regrettably, there was no single basic action open to me on Saturday such that, had I performed it, I would thereby have made it the case that I had ten pages of notes by Sunday evening.

In light of this sort of observation, one might try the following:

$O_{st} p$ if and only if
there are times $t_1 \ldots t_n$, not earlier than t, and basic action types $A_1 \ldots A_n$, such that:
(a) $O_{st} A_1 (s, t_1) \& \ldots \& O_{st} A (s, t_n)$ and
(b) had S done A_1 at $t_1, \ldots$, and A_n at t_n, then S would thereby have made it the case that p.

But this will not quite do either. It does not give us a sufficient condition. It is, we may suppose, now open to me to do a push-up within the next ten seconds and also now open to me to do a push-up within the ten seconds after the next ten seconds, and so on for, say, each of the next sixty successive ten-second intervals. And if I were to do all those push-ups in all those ten-second intervals, then I would make it the case that by ten minutes from now I have done sixty push-ups. But from these suppositions, it does not follow that it is now open to me to make it the case that I do sixty push-ups in the next ten minutes. The unfortunate fact is that were I to do the first several push-ups (considerably fewer than sixty), I would thereby cause myself to lose the power to do any more (for a while). So we need to include in part (a) the proviso that actually performing all of an initial part of the sequence would leave it at that later point still open to one to perform the next action in the sequence.[24]

So we end up with the following rather complicated-looking analysis:

$O_{st} p$ if and only if
there are times $t_1 \ldots t_n$ (ordered from earlier to later), not earlier than t, and basic action types $A_1 \ldots A_n$ such that
(a) $O_{st} A_1 (s, t_1)$ and
     had S done A_1 at t_1, then $O_{st2} A_2 (s, t_2) \&$ had S done A_1

---

24 The need for such a proviso has been noted by others, for example, Chisholm (1976b, pp. 63–4).

at t_1 and A_2 at t_2, then $O_{st3}A_3(s, t_3)$ & ... & had S done A_1 at t_1, ... , and A_{n-1} at t_{n-1} then $O_{stn}A_n(s, t_n)$ and

(b) had S done A_1 at t_1, ... , and A_n at t_n, then S would thereby have made it the case that p.

6

Reasons explanation of action

The preceding chapter argued for incompatibilism. In this chapter, I want to rebut two arguments against incompatibilism that have been put forward from time to time. Incompatibilism can be defined this way: Any free action must be an undetermined event. A *free* action is one such that, until the time of its occurrence, the agent had it open to her to perform some alternative action (or to be inactive) instead. An *undetermined* event is one that was *not* nomically necessitated by the antecedent state of the world. (Hence, a determined event is one that *was* nomically necessitated by its antecedents.) An event was *nomically necessitated* by the antecedent state of the world if and only if the antecedent state together with the laws of nature determined that that event, rather than some alternative, would occur.

The most widely supported argument against incompatibilism, to which I will give by far the larger response, combines the consideration that a free action can be influenced by the agent's intentions, desires, and beliefs – can have an explanation in terms of reasons for which the agent did it – with the assumption that only a determined event can have such an explanation.[1] My response to this argument will be to counter the assumption by offering an adeterministic or *anomic* account of such explanations. The other argument does not assume that reasons explanations are deterministic (nor does it assume the contradictory), but simply claims that where we have an undetermined action we do not have an agent in control of (determining) what her action is to be: We do not have an action that the agent chooses, freely or otherwise.

---

1 The earliest appearance of this argument, or one closely akin to it, that I know of is in Hume's *Treatise*, bk. II, pt. III, sec. 2.

Let me first dispose of this latter argument. It is contained (though mingled with and not clearly distinguished from the other argument) in the following remarks of Frithjof Bergmann:

> Would indeterminacy, even if its existence could be demonstrated, really vouchsafe freedom, or would it not fulfill this expectation? . . . Where or when would [the indeterminacy] have to occur to provide us with freedom? . . . Imagine Raskolnikov walking up the steps to the old pawnbroker woman's room and assume that his mind still vacillates, that with every tread he climbs his thinking alternates from one side to the other. . . . he mounts the staircase thinking "I shall kill her," "no, I shall not." This continues till he stands right before her door. Now let us hypothesize that his last thought just as he pushes the door open is "no, I shall not do it" and that the sought-for indeterminacy occurs right after these words crossed his mind. The thinking of this thought is the last link in a causal chain, but now there is a gap between this and the next event, which is his bringing the axe down on her head.
>
> What would this mean? Would the occurrence of a disjuncture in this place render Raskolnikov's act more free; would it provide him with a power or a control that he lacks otherwise? . . . The implication, if anything, would be the reverse. If his last thought really is "no, I shall not do it" and this thought is somehow disconnected from the next event so that it has no causal influence on it and he then kills her, then one could only say that the indeterminacy has rendered his will ineffectual, that instead of giving him greater power or control the causal gap *decreased* it.
>
> . . . one could envision two alternatives: either something other than his own last thought "influences" him so that he does commit the murder, or the last reversal was quite strictly not effected by anything whatever and occurred entirely "by chance." . . . in either case it was not *he* that made the decision, and *he* certainly did not exercise his freedom. We therefore can conclude that the occurrence of a causal gap in this particular location – between his last thought and his action – would not furnish him with freedom, but on the contrary would undermine the agent and make him a victim.[2]

Bergmann is suggesting that there is an absurdity in the thought that positing a break in the causal necessitation just before Raskolnikov's action helps to make it one that *he* chooses. In fact, he suggests, it would do just the opposite: It would go against its being the case that Raskolnikov determines whether or not he delivers the murder-

---

2 Bergmann (1977, pp. 234–5). This is the central argument in an appendix titled "Freedom and Determinism".

ing blow. And if Raskolnikov does not determine that, then surely his delivering the blow is not his freely chosen action for which he can be held morally responsible.

Why exactly is the indeterminacy just before the action supposed to deprive the agent of control over his action? One reason, Bergmann seems to suggest, is that (as he thinks) if the action is undetermined, then it is in no way influenced by his antecedent intentions or thoughts, and its being influenced by them is essential to its being controlled by the agent. But his words, particularly the last few sentences quoted, also invite the thought that the implication is more direct and does not depend on taking a deterministic view of how motives influence actions or on taking any particular view of what agent control consists in: It is, one may think, just obvious that if an action is undetermined, then the agent does not control (determine) it, has no say in whether or not it occurs.

We also find this latter idea in the argument that van Inwagen (1983) refers to as "the third strand of the *Mind* Argument" for compatibilism. The premise of that argument, as van Inwagen phrases it (p. 144), is "the principle that no one has any choice about the occurrence of an undetermined event". I believe that we adequately capture the idea here if we express it as follows:

1. For any time t and any undetermined event occurring at t: It is not possible for it to have been open to anyone to determine whether that event or some alternative (undetermined) event instead would occur at t.

From this premise, we can in two short steps derive a conclusion severely damaging to incompatibilism:

2. Therefore, for any time t and any undetermined action occurring at t: It is not possible for it to have been open to the agent to determine whether that action or some alternative (undetermined) action instead would occur at t.
3. Therefore, it is not possible for a free action to be undetermined.

It is impossible for 3 and incompatibilism both to be true *if* it is also true that free action is at least possible (whether or not actual). The metaphysical possibility of free action is something that most incompatibilists assume, myself included, as, of course, do most compatibilists. That assumption, conjoined with 3, does entail that incompatibilism is false. Since the argument is obviously valid, if free action is possible, either incompatibilism or the argument's premise is wrong. A little reflection will show us that the latter is the problem.

126

Whatever plausibility this premise has derives, I think, from ambiguity in sentences of the following form when they are about events that are actions.

(A)   It was open to S to determine whether undetermined event E or some alternative undetermined event instead would occur at t.

When event E is *not an action of S's*, a natural reading of this sentence does make it express a plainly impossible proposition:

(A1)   It was open to S so to act that S's action (in concert with other circumstances at the time) would have nomically necessitated that E would occur at t and would have been undetermined; and it was open to S so to act that S's action would have nomically necessitated that some alternative instead of E would occur at t and would have been undetermined.

Here each conjunct is impossible, for it implies that it was open to S to make the case something that is logically impossible, namely, that an event at t would have been both determined and undetermined. On this inconsistent reading of (A), the premise of the argument, 1 earlier, obviously holds.

But when event E is an action of S's, another reading of (A) is possible, one that is perfectly consistent:

(A2)   It was open to S to act in a certain way at t without being nomically necessitated to do so; and it was open to S to act in some alternative way at t without being nomically necessitated to do so.

Here each conjunct says that it was open to S to make the case something that in itself is perfectly possible, namely, S's performing an undetermined action. If an undetermined action is possible, then there is no reason to say that an undetermined action cannot be open to the agent to perform.

To determine an event is to act in such a way that one's action makes it the case that the event occurs. Let us grant (for the sake of this discussion) that if the event is *not* one's own action, then this requires that the event be causally necessitated by one's action (in concert with other circumstances) and thus that it not be an undetermined event. But if the event *is* one's own action, then one's determining it requires only that one perform it; and one's performing it, which is just the action's occurring, is compatible with that event's being undetermined, not causally necessitated by antecedents.

Suppose that S's raising her arm at t did occur as an undetermined action: S raised her arm at t without being nomically necessitated to do so. In that case, it was open to S up to t to raise her arm at t

127

without being nomically necessitated to do so. There is no reason to doubt it. Nor is there any reason to be puzzled as to how this can be so. But van Inwagen (in uncomfortable company with some compatibilists) seems to find a mystery here. He says:

I must reject the following proposition:
>   If an agent's act was caused but not determined by his prior inner state, and if nothing besides that inner state was causally relevant to the agent's act, then that agent had no choice about whether that inner state was followed by that act.

I must admit that I find it puzzling that this proposition should be false. . . .

Now I wish I knew *how it could be* that, for example, our thief had a choice about whether to repent [or instead rob the poor box], given that his repenting was caused, but not determined, by his prior inner states, and given that no other prior state "had anything to do with" – save negatively: in virtue of its non-interference with – his act. I have no theory of free action or choice that would explain how this could be.[3]

As I understand him, what puzzles van Inwagen is how an agent could have a choice about whether or not his action occurred, that is, could determine that it occurred rather than something else instead, *if* the only antecedent things causally relevant to its occurrence, the agent's motives for it (his "prior inner state"), left it undetermined, nomically unnecessitated. How, by what means, van Inwagen seems to want to ask, did the thief ensure that that action (rather than some alternative) occurred? The answer is: by no *means,* by nothing distinct from and productive of the action, but simply by performing the action itself. If an event is S's action, then S (but, of course, no one else) can ensure its occurrence, determine *that* it occurs and thus *whether or not* it occurs, just by performing it.

So I attribute the puzzlement van Inwagen feels here to failure to distinguish the two very different readings sentences of form (A) can have when E is one of S's own actions. He wants to say that (A) can be true in such a case, but he wonders *how* it can be. His feeling that (A) can be true is traceable to the $(A2)$ interpretation, which gives a proposition whose possibility is clear and straightforward. His conflicting feeling that there is no way (A) can be true in such a case is traceable to the $(A1)$ interpretation, which gives an inconsistent proposition.

---

3 Van Inwagen (1983, pp. 149–50).

Let us turn now to the other argument against incompatibilism I mentioned earlier. This one crucially assumes that if an action is not a purely chance or random event, if it is influenced by or has an explanation in terms of the agent's reasons or motives for doing it, then it is ipso facto determined. A. J. Ayer (1946), for instance, says:

Either it is an accident that I choose to act as I do or it is not. If it is an accident, then it is merely a matter of chance that I did not choose otherwise; and if it is merely a matter of chance that I did not choose otherwise, it is surely irrational to hold me morally responsible for choosing as I did. But if it is not an accident that I choose to do one thing rather than another, then presumably there is some causal explanation of my choice: and in that case we are led back to determinism.[4]

J. J. C. Smart (1968) argues that

the question of pure chance or determinism is irrelevant to the question of free will, though, so far from free will and determinism being incompatible with one another, a close approximation to determinism on the macro-level is required for free will.

Some philosophers would ... say that in free choice we act from reasons, not from causes, and they would say that acting from reasons is neither caused nor a matter of pure chance. I find this unintelligible.

... the free choice is supposed to be not deterministic and not a matter of pure chance. It is supposed to be pure chance in the sense of "not being determined" but the suggestion is that it is also not merely random and is "acting from reasons". The previous paragraph [not quoted here; see footnote 15 for a description of its content] suggests, however, that acting from reasons is not merely random precisely because it is also acting from causes.[5]

We can formulate the argument these authors make as follows:

1. Incompatibilism entails that an action cannot be both free and determined by an antecedent state of the world.
2. If an action is not determined by an antecedent state of the world, then it has no explanation in terms of its antecedents.
3. But some free actions do have explanations in terms of their antecedents.
4. Therefore, incompatibilism is wrong.

Premise 1 is true by the definition of incompatibilism. Premise 3 is obviously undeniable. We frequently give explanations of

---

4 Ayer (1959, p. 275).
5 Smart (1968, pp. 300–1).

our own actions, and accept explanations of others' actions, like the following:

> S opened the window in order to let the smoke out.
> S wanted to get out of the country quickly and realized that it would take days unless she gave the official a bribe, so she handed him all her cash.

These are explanations of actions because they answer the question "Why did S do that?" The first explains why S opened the window. The second explains why S handed the official all her cash. These examples illustrate a category of explanations that apply only to actions: They are explanations that give us the agent's reasons for acting as she did. For most of our actions, or most that we have occasion to reflect on, we believe that they have such reasons explanations. Very often some of the intentions, desires, or beliefs that we bring into such an explanation are antecedents of the action. It would be preposterous to suggest that free actions can never have such explanations, to deny premise 3.

Some philosophers seem to think that premise 3 would be acceptable even if it were stronger and said that an action *must* have an explanation in terms of its antecedents, or that this must be true of *responsible* actions or of ones that the agent *chooses,* ones that are truly the agent's actions. Bergmann, for example, seems to suggest this in the remarks quoted earlier. But I can see no reason to accept these much stronger claims. When I cross my legs while listening to a lecture, that action (usually) has no explanation in terms of reasons for doing it that I had antecedently. I just spontaneously do it. A spontaneous action, not arising from any antecedent motive, can even be undertaken with a further intention that begins to exist just when the action does. For example, a bird catches a person's eye and, without having antecedently formed the intention to keep watching it, she moves her head when the bird moves in order to keep her eyes on it.

But premise 3 itself is obviously true. As I said, it would be absurd to suppose that a free action could not have an explanation in terms of the agent's antecedent reasons for doing it. It is premise 2, that an action has no explanation in terms of its antecedents if it is not determined by them, that is the substantive and deniable premise in the argument. Ayer clearly assumes that there are only two alternatives: Either an action is determined or it is a purely chance event. He says, "if it is not an accident that I choose to do one thing rather than another, then presumably there is some causal explanation of my choice: and in that case we are led back to determinism." Smart finds unintelligible the suggestion that there is a third alternative, "that acting from reasons is neither caused [determined] nor a matter of pure chance."

To assume premise 2 is to assume that *all* explanations of events must be law governed or *nomic*. That is to assume that an explanation can be true only if laws of nature guarantee that the explaining factors plus other circumstances are accompanied by the explained event. Applied specifically to reasons explanations of actions, this means the following:

(B)   A reasons explanation can be true only if laws of nature guarantee that the agent's reasons for performing the action plus other circumstances are accompanied by the explained action.

This bold, bald assumption is false.

LAWS GOVERNING REASONS EXPLANATIONS ARE NOT KNOWN

Some philosophers have thought that the laws of nature that govern reasons explanations in the way required by assumption (B) are fairly obvious. J. S. Mill, for example, in his *Examination of Sir William Hamilton's Philosophy,* says that "Necessitarians", of whom he counts himself one,

affirm, as a truth of experience, that volitions do, in point of fact, follow determinate moral antecedents with the same uniformity, and (when we have sufficient knowledge of the circumstances) with the same certainty, as physical effects follow their physical causes. These moral antecedents are desires, aversions, habits, and dispositions, combined with outward circumstances suited to call those internal incentives into action. . . . A volition is a moral effect, which follows the corresponding moral causes as certainly and invariably as physical effects follow their physical causes.[6]

One may object that, in point of fact, the same volition or action does not invariably follow the same set of "moral" antecedents, and this is particularly clear in cases (which are common) where the moral antecedents include the agent's having two or more desires that conflict, so that the agent can satisfy at most one of these desires. For example, on a Saturday afternoon I have a desire to spend the rest of the afternoon doing some philosophical work and also a

6 Mill (1872, pp. 449–50).

131

desire to spend it watching a football game on television. Suppose that this same set of conflicting motives recurs on several Saturday afternoons. Can't I choose to satisfy one of the motives on some of these occasions and the other on other occasions, without there being any relevant difference in the antecedents on these several occasions? Mill says no.

> When we think of ourselves hypothetically as having acted otherwise than we did, we always suppose a difference in the antecedents: we picture ourselves as having known something that we did not know, or not known something that we did know; which is a difference in the external inducements; or as having desired something, or disliked something, more or less than we did; which is a difference in the internal inducements.[7]

It is already clear to Mill what the general law must be in such cases of conflict of motives: The chosen action will be the one that satisfies whichever of the conflicting motives is stronger than all the others: The strongest motive prevails.[8]

Thomas Reid (writing more than sixty years before Mill) makes the following remarks about this way of dealing with conflict-of-motives cases:

> When it is said, that of contrary motives the strongest always prevails, this can neither be affirmed nor denied with understanding, until we know distinctly what is meant by the strongest motive . . . when the motives are of different kinds, as money and fame, duty and worldly interest, health and strength, riches and honor, by what rule shall we judge which is the strongest motive? Either we measure the strength of motives, merely by their prevalence, or by some other standard distinct from their prevalence. If we measure their strength merely by their prevalence, and by the strongest motive mean only the motive that prevails, it will be true indeed that the strongest motive prevails; but the proposition will be identical, and mean no more than that the strongest motive is the strongest motive. From this surely no conclusion can be drawn. . . . We are therefore brought to this issue, that unless some measure of the strength of motives can be found distinct from their prevalence, it cannot be determined, whether the strongest motive always prevails or not. If such a measure can be found and applied, we may be able to judge of the truth of this maxim, but not otherwise.[9]

This suggests that one can secure confidence in Mill's law only by making it true by definition: The "strongest motive" *means* the motive that prevails. If this term is defined by some logically independent criterion, so that the proposed law will be a nontrivial

---

7 Mill (1872, p. 451).
8 See Mill (1872, pp. 451–3).
9 Reid (1815), quoted from Dworkin ed. (1970, pp. 88–9).

proposition, then it is an open question whether the facts would give us reason for confidence in it. Reid presents Mill with a dilemma: Either the strongest motive law is true by definition, in which case it is not the law of nature that was wanted, or some independent test of the strongest motive is to be found, in which case we do not know yet whether the proposed law holds.

Mill attempts to reply to this line of thought. He says that there are two flaws in the argument that "I only know the strength of motives in relation to the will by the test of ultimate prevalence; so that this means no more than that the prevailing motive prevails."

First, those who say that the will follows the strongest motive, do not mean the motive which is strongest in relation to the will, or in other words, that the will follows what it does follow. They mean the motive which is strongest in relation to pain and pleasure; since a motive, being a desire or aversion, is proportional to the pleasantness, as conceived by us, of the thing desired, or the painfulness of the thing shunned. . . . The second [flaw] is, that even supposing there were no test of the strength of motives but their effect on the will, the proposition that the will follows the strongest motive would not . . . be identical and unmeaning. We say, without absurdity, that if two weights are placed in opposite scales, the heavier will lift the other up; yet we mean nothing by the heavier, except the weight which will lift up the other. The proposition, nevertheless, is not unmeaning, for it signifies that in many or most cases there *is* a heavier, and that this is always the same one, not one or the other as it may happen. In like manner, even if the strongest motive meant only the motive which prevails, yet if there is a prevailing motive – if, all other antecedents being the same, the motive which prevails today will prevail tomorrow and every subsequent day – Sir W. Hamilton was acute enough to see that the free-will theory is not saved.[10]

This fails to wriggle out of the dilemma. Mill's proposed independent criterion of motive strength is the degree of pain and pleasure anticipated. On any ordinary understanding of this, the facts will not support the proposed law: People sometimes choose an alternative that they believe will be more painful or less pleasant than another alternative they believe open to them – in order to keep a promise, for example. In his second point, Mill seems to give the game away, apparently without quite realizing it. He says that even if there were no other test of the strongest motive but the one that prevails, this would make the strongest motive law no more absurd and unmeaning than "the heaviest weight always lifts the other up".

10 Mill (1872, pp. 468–9).

133

To this Reid should reply: Exactly so. No more unmeaning *and no less tautologous.*

Mill goes on to claim that the proposition "The heavier weight lifts the other up" "signifies that in many or most cases there is a heavier *and this is always the same one,* not one or the other as it may happen" (emphasis added). He implies that the corresponding proposition, "The strongest motive prevails", implies a corresponding thing, that the prevailing motive in recurrences of the same set of conflicting motives is always the same one. But, of course, neither tautology can have the implication claimed for it. It is a contingent proposition, and therefore compatible with "the heavier weight lifts the other up", that two objects should change over time with respect to which is the heavier of the two. Likewise it is contingent, and therefore compatible with the tautological interpretation of "the strongest motive prevails", that when the same set of conflicting motives recurs, a different one prevails from the one that prevailed earlier. And, more important, this is not only a logical possibility but actually happens, often. Sometimes when my desire to work conflicts with my desire to watch football the first motive prevails, and sometimes the second prevails. Sometimes when my desire to get an early start on the day conflicts with my desire to sleep a bit more the first desire prevails, and sometimes the second does. If there are laws of nature that explain why the prevailing motive does prevail in such cases, that explain this in terms of antecedents of the action, it is far from obvious what the contents of those laws are and it seems unlikely that they deal entirely in terms of moral antecedents (that is, the agent's antecedent reasons or motives), for it seems that we already know all the relevant facts about them: The agent had the conflicting motives, and it seemed a tossup which one to satisfy.

There is another sort of case, noted by Reid, where the strongest motive law cannot apply at all, even on its tautological interpretation, because there is no motive that distinguishes the chosen alternative from another one.[11] On my computer's keyboard there are two keys such that if I press either of them the result is that an asterisk appears on the screen. I know this about these keys and I want to produce an asterisk, so I have a motive or reason for pressing one of them. Now suppose further that I have no desire such that

11 See Dworkin ed. (1970, p. 87), excerpted from Reid (1815).

pressing one but not the other of these two keys satisfies it. I have no motive for pressing one of them that is not also equally a motive for pressing the other. I am utterly indifferent between these two equally good means to my end of putting an asterisk on the screen. So I arbitrarily choose to press one of them. Here we cannot say that my pressing one rather than the other signified the prevailing of one over another of two conflicting motives that I had. There *were no* conflicting motives such that one motive favored one key and the other motive favored the other key. Yet I did press the key I pressed for a reason, namely, in order to produce an asterisk. The answer to "Why did he press that key?" is "Because he wanted to produce an asterisk".

Of course, I did not have a reason for pressing that key *rather than the other*. There is no answer to "Why did he press that key rather than this other one?", at least no answer that is a reasons explanation. I chose to press that key for a certain reason, but it is not the case that I had a reason for *not* pressing the other one instead. A similar situation holds in a conflict-of-motives case where it seems to the agent a tossup which motive to satisfy. The answer to "Why did he get out of bed just then?" is "Because he wanted to get an early start on his day". But to the question "Why did he get out of bed rather than stay in it and enjoy a bit more sleep?" there may be no answer, because there may be no answer to "Why did he choose to get an early start rather than to get more sleep?".

In this case, it is plausible to suppose that, *if* there is a *nomic* explanation of why he got out of bed rather than remaining in it, his desire to get an early start will figure in it, since it was a reason for that action but not a reason for the alternative. Of course, it cannot be the only relevant antecedent in a nomic explanation here, and the available reasons explanation affords little hint as to what might be the other antecedents that would subsume the case under laws of nature. In the indifferent means case, however, we have no good reason to suppose that, if there is a nomic explanation of why I pressed one key rather than the other one, my motive for pressing that key will figure in it, since it was an equally good motive for the other alternative. It seems that here the available reasons explanation for my action gives little hint as to what the antecedents of this nomic explanation might be if there is one.

So, contrary to what Mill appears to suggest, our reasons explanations for our actions do not always show us, or even give us much of a clue to, what the laws are (if any) that govern the determination of our actions by their antecedents.

But to show that we do not know the causal laws governing our reasons explanations is not to show that no such laws obtain[12] or that their obtaining would be incompatible with the reasons explanations. Some philosophers have tried to make this latter claim of incompatibility,[13] but their arguments do not succeed, as Davidson (1963), among others, has shown.[14] But that issue is not relevant here, for assumption (B) makes a much stronger claim than that a reasons explanation of an action is *compatible* with the action's being nomically necessitated by its antecedents. Assumption (B) is that reasons explanations *require* such necessitation. That is something that Davidson (1963) does *not* argue for but simply assumes.[15] Neither does Ayer or Smart argue for this requirement. Smart writes as if he has done so when he says, "The previous paragraph suggests . . . that acting from reasons is not merely random precisely because it is also acting from causes", but in the paragraph he refers to, he argues only that reasons explanations *can* be nomic.[16] That is not the same thing. The possibility of nomic reasons explanations does not imply the impossibility of anomic reasons explanations.

There are arguments that might be given for assumption (B). It might be said, for instance, that in giving a reasons explanation we are giving *causes* of the action – we do frequently use the word *because* in giving reasons explanations – and where there are causes there

---

12 As Davidson (1963) points out.
13 For example, Melden (1961) and Malcolm (1968).
14 See Goldman (1969), which focuses on Malcolm (1968).
15 As he does, for example, in this remark (reprinted in Davidson, 1980, p. 17): "*The laws whose existence is required if reasons are causes of actions* do not, we may be sure, deal in the concepts in which rationalizations must deal" (emphasis mine). Davidson's view about reasons explanation, more fully spelled out in Davidson (1970), is that the truth of such an explanation requires that there be ways of "redescribing" the reasons explanans and the action-or-decision explanandum in neurological or chemical or physical terms that (presumably along with similar descriptions of other circumstances) instantiate a law.
16 Smart (1968, p. 300) argues that a computer programmed to select items from a set according to certain criteria can be said to have been "programmed to act in accordance with what we would call 'good reasons' ".

must be nomic necessitation. But this last premise amounts to just another way of stating assumption (*B*). A more worthy argument is this: In any explanation of an event in terms of its antecedents, there must be some relation between explanans and explanandum in virtue of which the one explains the other. What else could this explanatory connection be if it is not that the explanans plus other antecedent circumstances nomically necessitate the explanandum?

That is a fair question. We can show that the right answer is *not* "There is nothing else it could be" by showing that for paradigm reasons explanations there are conditions that

> are obviously sufficient for their truth,
> obviously do not entail that there is any true law covering the case (any nomic explanation of the action), but
> do involve another sort of obviously explanatory connection between the explained action and its explanans.

Any condition satisfying these criteria I will call an *anomic* sufficient condition for a reasons explanation. It is not difficult to specify such conditions.

Consider first a very simple sort of reasons explanation, the sort expressed in a sentence of one of the following forms:[17]

(1) a. *S V*-ed in order (thereby) to *U*.
     b. By *V*-ing *S* intended to *U*.
     c. *S V*-ed with the intention of (thereby) *U*-ing.

I take these different forms to give us different ways of saying the same thing.[18] Some instances of these forms are as follows:

> *S* rubbed her hands together in order to warm them up.
> By flipping the switch, *S* intended to turn on the light.
> *S* opened the window with the intention of letting out the smoke.

---

17 In these forms, "*V*-ed" is a variable ranging over past-tense singular forms of action verb phrases (for example, "opened the door"), "to *U*" ranges over infinitive forms ("to open the door"), and "*V*-ing" ranges over progressive forms minus their auxiliaries ("opening the door").

18 Certainly, (1b) and (1c) are equivalent and each implies (1a), and in normal sorts of cases where (1a) is true (1b–c) will be true also. But, as we noted in Chapter 4, Bratman (1987, ch. 8) has pointed out that there are unusual sorts of cases where it seems right to say that (1a) is true but (1b–c) are not, given the plausible assumption that, if one believes that ends *E*1 and *E*2 cannot both be achieved, one cannot (without being criticizably irrational) intend to achieve both, but one can both undertake action *A*1 in order to achieve (aiming at achieving) *E*1 and undertake action *A*2 in order to achieve *E*2.

A statement of any of the forms (1a–c) is an answer to the question "Why did S V?"; it offers an explanation of S's V-ing. It says that S's reason for V-ing was that she believed and intended that by V-ing she would U. Actually, "believed and intended" is redundant. S's intending that by V-ing she would U implies that S believes that by V-ing she has enough chance of U-ing to make V-ing worth the effort, and that is all the belief that the explanation requires. So we can say that such an explanation says that S's reason (or at least one of S's reasons) for V-ing was her intention thereby to U.

The only thing *required* for the truth of a reasons explanation of this sort, besides the occurrence of the explained action, is that the action have been *accompanied* by an intention with the right sort of content. Specifically, given that S did V, it will suffice for the truth of "S V-ed in order to U" if the following condition obtains:

(C1)   Concurrently with her action of V-ing, S intended by *that* action to U (S intended *of* that action that by it she would U).

If from its inception S intended of her action of opening the window that by performing it she would let in fresh air (from its inception she had the intention that she could express with the sentence "I am undertaking this opening of the window in order to let in fresh air"), then ipso facto it was her purpose in that action to let in fresh air; she did it in order to let in fresh air.

This is so even in the possible case where there is also true some independent explanation of the action in terms other than the agent's reasons. Imagine that by direct electronic manipulation of neural events in S (through, say, electrodes implanted in the part of S's brain that controls voluntary bodily exertion), someone else caused S voluntarily to open a window. Now the (C1) condition (where V is "open the window" and U is "let in fresh air") could also be true in such a case. The accompanying intention required by (C1) is at least conceptually compatible with the direct manipulation of S's voluntary exertions by another. Indeed, there appears to be nothing incoherent in the supposition that the controllers of the implanted electrodes might arrange to produce both S's voluntary exertion and the accompanying intention about it. If the (C1) condition were also true, then it would be the case that S intended by opening the window to let in fresh air. So it would be the case that S opened the window because of the other's manipulation of S's brain events *and* S opened the window in order to let in fresh air. There is no reason to think that the truth of either explanation must preclude the truth of the other.

Note that the content of the intention specified in (C1) refers *directly* to the action it is an intention about. That is, it does not refer to that particular action via a description of it but rather, as it were, demonstratively. The content of the intention is not the proposition "There is now exactly one action of V-ing by me, and by it I shall U" but rather the proposition "By *this* V-ing (of which I am now aware) I shall U".[19] It is owing to this direct reference that the intention is about, and thus explanatory of, *that particular* action.

Such an intention, which is directly about a particular action, could not begin before the particular action does. In general, whether the propositional attitude be intending or believing or desiring or any other, for the proposition involved to contain a direct or demonstrative reference to a particular requires that the particular have an appropriate sort of role in causing whatever constitutes the reference to it, a relation that is precluded if the reference comes before the particular begins to exist. (It is enough if the particular has begun to exist, even if it is an event: One can demonstratively refer to a particular event by demonstratively referring to a part of it.) This means that we have a factor, the agent's concurrently intending something of the action, that is sufficient to verify a reasons explanation of the action and that not only does not but could not precede the action. We have a sufficient condition that entails nothing about what happened before the action that is relevant to explaining it. We have a reasons explanation that is entirely in terms of a concurrent state or process and not at all in terms of any antecedent one.

Usually, some explanatory antecedent is in the background of this sort of reasons explanation, "S V-ed in order to U". Usually, the intention concurrent with S's V-ing is the outcome of an antecedent intention, or at least desire, to U in the very near future. Usually, maybe even always, when an agent opens a window in order to let in fresh air, or pushes on a door in order to open it, she has already formed the intention to perform such an action for such

---

19 Wilson (1980, ch. V) calls attention to such directly referring intentions. He calls them *act-relational* intentions and contrasts them with *future action* intentions. To be exact, it is the statements attributing these two kinds of intentions, rather than the intentions themselves, that he calls *act-relational* and *future action*. An act-relational statement attributes, as he puts it, an intention *with which* the agent acts, an intention the agent has *in* the action.

an end and the action is undertaken in order to carry out that antecedently formed intention, or at least she antecedently possessed a desire for that end and the action is undertaken in order to satisfy that antecedently existing desire. But, however common it may be, there is no necessity that it be so: One can quite spontaneously do such things with such intentions.

So we see that our sufficient condition for explanations of sort (1), in terms of a concurrent intention regarding the particular action, does not entail that the action has a nomic explanation in terms of its antecedents. We should also see that it does not entail that the action has a nomic explanation in terms of concurrent conditions. Of course, the following generalization is true of such cases: For any agent S and time t, if S intends of her V-ing at t that she thereby U, then S Vs at t. But this is logically necessary and not a law of nature. It may be, of course, that when S has an intention directly about a current action of hers, intends of *this* V-ing that by it she U, there is a mental state of S that is necessary for her having this intention but is compatible with the nonoccurrence of the action of V-ing, a mental state that needs to be supplemented only by the right relation to the action for the whole to be her intending something *of* that action. But it will not be plausible to suppose that it is a law of nature that whenever an agent has this sort of mental state – ingredient in intending something of a concurrent V-ing but compatible with there being no V-ing – she does concurrently V. There is certainly no nomic necessity that her belief of her concurrent action that it is a V-ing be true. Even where that belief logically could not be false (as might plausibly be held for the case where V-ing is a mental act of volition), there is no case for saying that our sufficient condition entails a nomic connection. Either there is an ingredient of the agent's direct intention about her V-ing that is compatible with her not V-ing or there is no such ingredient. If the latter, then the intention does not give us the nonentailing condition necessary for a nomic explanation. If the former, then, although this aspect *could* be part of a nomically necessitating factor, there is nothing in the condition itself that entails that it must be so. There is, we have noted, a causal connection between the action and the intention required for the latter to refer directly to the former. But even if this must involve a nomic connection – and it is by no means clear that it must – the causation goes in the wrong direction, from explained action to explaining intention rather than the other way around. (In general, when one's thought contains a direct reference to a particular, it is in virtue of the particular's producing something in the thought, not vice versa.)

If the explanatory connection between the explaining intention and the explained action is not nomic necessitation, then what is it? Well, it stares one in the face. In reasons explanations of sort (1), the concurrent intention explains the action simply in virtue of being an intention of that action that by or in it the agent will do a certain thing, in virtue, that is, of being that sort of propositional attitude (an intention) whose content has that feature (its being that by or in that action a certain thing will be done). That is all there is to it. It is simple, but for the purpose of explaining the action it is sufficient. Aside from the relation required for the direct reference, this is an *internal* relation between the explaining factor and the explained action. It follows from the direct reference plus *intrinsic* properties of the relata, namely, the property of one that it is an action of S's and the property of the other that it is an intention of S's with a certain sort of content, namely, that the item to which it directly refers be an action with such and such properties. The explanatory connection is made not by laws of nature but by the direct reference and the internal relation.

Are reasons explanations of sort (1) *causal* explanations? They are if all one means by *causal* is that the explanation can be expressed with a *because* linking the explanandum and the explanans. ("She opened the window because she intended thereby to let out the smoke.") If, on the other hand, one requires that a cause, properly so called, precede its effect, then these are not causal explanations. And it perhaps sounds odd to speak of a *concurrent* intention about an action as *causing* or *producing* or *resulting in* or *leading to* the action.

None of these expressions sounds odd, however, when speaking of a motive or reason the agent had prior to the action. One case where the explaining factor is antecedent to the action is the case where we explain the action as the carrying out of a decision the agent had made, an intention she had formed. One class of such explanations is expressible by sentences of the following form:

(2) a. S V-ed then in order to carry out her intention to V when F.
   b. S V-ed then because she had intended to V when F and she believed it was then F.

Here (2b) simply spells out more fully what (2a) implies. Some examples of this sort of explanation are as follows:

> S opened the window in order to carry out her intention to
> open the window when people started smoking.
> S raised her hand in order to carry out her intention to raise it
> as soon as the chair called for the votes in favor of the motion.

What is an anomic sufficient condition for the truth of such an explanation? The wording of (2a) suggests that it should include, besides the explained action and the antecedent intention, an intention concurrent with the action to the effect that the action is a carrying out of the prior intention. This will make it the case that S performed the action *in order* to carry out that prior intention, performed it, that is, with the intention of carrying out that prior intention. So we can say that an explanation of sort (2) is true if (C2) is true.

(C2)   (a) Prior to this V-ing, S had an intention to V when F, and (b) concurrently with this V-ing, S remembered that prior intention and its content and intended of this V-ing that it carry out that prior intention (be a V-ing when F).

Note that S cannot have the concurrent intention specified in (C2b) without believing that F now obtains; so it guarantees the second conjunct of (2b).

It is obvious that this sufficient condition is anomic. That is, it is obviously compatible with the truth of (C2) in a particular case of S's V-ing that there should be another case (involving S or some other agent) that is exactly similar in everything antecedent to the action (including other circumstances as well as the agent's intention to V) but lacks the agent's V-ing. Thus (C2) could hold even if there were no nomic explanation of S's V-ing in terms of the prior intention plus other antecedent circumstances. What then makes the explanatory connection here, if it is not a nomic connection? Well, in the concurrent intention required by (C2), S intends of her current action that it be of just the sort specified in the content of the required prior intention (to which the content of the concurrent intention must refer), namely, a V-ing when F. It is this internal and referential relation between the contents of the prior and the concurrent intention, together with the explanatory relation of the concurrent intention to the action, which we have already discussed, that makes the explanatory connection between the prior intention and the action. The connection has two links, from prior to concurrent intention and from concurrent intention to action.

Following the model of (C2) for explanations of sort (2), it is not difficult to work out anomic sufficient conditions for other forms of reasons explanations in terms of antecedent states of the agent. Consider, for example, the sort expressed by sentences of the following form:

(3) a. S V-ed in order to carry out her (antecedent) intention to U.
   b. S V-ed because she had intended to U and believed that by V-ing she would (or might) U.

Here (3b) spells out more fully what is implied by (3a). Some examples of instances of this form of explanation are as follows:

> S shouted in order to carry out her (antecedent) intention to frighten away any bears that might be in the vicinity.
> S said, "They're gone," because she had intended to let R know when they had gone and believed that by saying that she would (or might) do so.

The following is an anomic sufficient condition for the truth of explanations of sort (3).

(C3)   (a) Prior to V-ing, S had the intention to U, and (b) concurrently with V-ing, S remembered that prior intention and intended that by this V-ing she would carry it out.

S's having the concurrent intention specified in (C3b) requires that S believe that by this V-ing she would or might U, and thus it entails the second conjunct of (3b).

Still another sort of reasons explanation in terms of antecedents is expressible in sentences of the following form:

(4) S V-ed because she had desired that p and believed that by V-ing she would (or might) make it the case that p (or contribute to doing so).

Examples of this sort of explanation are as follows:

> S opened the window because she had a desire for fresher air in the room and believed that opening the window would let in fresher air.
> S voted for the motion because she wanted it to pass and believed that her vote would (or might) help it to do so.

The following gives an anomic sufficient condition for explanations of this sort:

(C4)   (a) Prior to V-ing, S had a desire that p, and (b) concurrently with V-ing, S remembered that prior desire and intended of this V-ing that it satisfy (or contribute to satisfying) that desire.

Our anomic sufficient conditions for explanations of actions in terms of antecedent reasons, (C2) to (C4), require S to remember the prior mental state (of intention or desire) while engaged in the action that that prior state explains. This is a feature of any ano-mic sufficient condition for a reasons explanation of an action in terms of a prior state of the agent. If at the time the agent begins the action she has no memory at all of the prior desire or intention, then it can hardly be a factor motivating that action. Now it is not necessary in order for (C4), for example, to be an anomic sufficient condition for the truth of (4) that this memory connection be ano-mic as well. Even if it were true that there is remembering of the prior desire only if there is a nomic connection between the prior state (plus its circumstances) and some current state, it would not follow from this and (C4) that there must be a nomic connection between the prior desire (plus its circumstances) and the action for which, given the truth of (C4), it provides a reasons explanation. But it is interesting to note, incidentally, that it is possible to specify an anomic sufficient condition for remembering, for the connection between an earlier state of mind and a later one, that makes the latter a memory of the former. S's seeming to remember a prior intention to do such and such is a memory of a particular prior in-tention *if* S had such a prior intention and nothing independent of that prior intention has happened sufficient to produce S's seem-ing to remember such an intention. More generally, one's having had prior experience of a certain sort is the *default* explanation of one's later seeming to remember having had such experience, in the sense that it is the explanation *unless* this role is preempted by something else, independent of it, that was sufficient to cause the memory impression.[20]

Like those in terms of concurrent intentions, our anomic suf-ficient conditions for reasons explanations in terms of antecedent motives are compatible with the truth of independent explanations in terms other than the agent's reasons. Consider again our example of S's voluntarily opening a window *both* as a result of another's ma-nipulation of events in S's brain *and* in order to let in fresh air. Add to it that S had earlier formed a desire for fresher air in the room and, concurrently with her opening the window, remembered that desire and intended of that action that it satisfy that desire, making true the appropriate instance of (C4). Then you have a case where S opened the window both because of the signals sent to the voli-tional part of her brain and in order to satisfy her antecedent desire.

20 I have argued this point more fully in Ginet (1975, pp. 160–5).

144

Again, there is no reason to think that the truth of either explanation excludes the truth of the other.

A noteworthy fact about (C4), the anomic sufficient condition for an explanation of the form "S V-ed because she had desired that p and believed that by V-ing she would satisfy that desire", is that it suggests a way of distinguishing between (1) a desire that was a reason for which the agent acted as she did and (2) a desire that was *not* a reason for which the agent acted as she did, although it was a reason for so acting that the agent was aware of having at the time. A desire of the agent's fits description (1) if the agent acts with the intention that that action satisfy that desire; and a desire of the agent's fits description (2) if, and only if, the agent has no such intention concurrent with the action despite being aware of the desire and of the fact that it is a reason for acting as she did (given her beliefs).

One may wonder, however, if and how there *could* be cases that fit description (2). Our account so far does not answer this question, but only turns it into the question of whether it could be that an agent at the time of acting believes that her action will satisfy a certain desire she has without intending of the action that it satisfy that desire. Suppose that S urgently needs her glasses, which she left in R's room, where R is now sleeping. S has some desire to wake R, because she would then have R's company, but also some desire *not* to wake R, because she knows that R needs the sleep. S decides to enter R's room in order to get her glasses, knowing as she does so that her action will satisfy her desire to wake R. Could it nevertheless be true that S did not intend of her action that it wake R? Bratman (1987) offers an illuminating account of how this could be so.[21] It seems right to say that S did not intend to wake R if S was so disposed that, had it turned out that her entering the room did not wake R, S would not have felt that her plan had failed to be completely realized, and she must then either wake R in some other way or decide to abandon part of her plan. And S's being thus

21 See Bratman (1987, pp. 155–60). The example he discusses differs from mine in that the agent in his example believes that the expected but unintended effect (the "side" effect) will help to achieve the same end that his intended means is intended to achieve, whereas in my example S does not believe this but desires the expected side effect, waking R, for reasons independent of her intended end, getting her glasses. But this difference seems immaterial to Bratman's account of how the side effect can, though expected and even desired (or believed to promote desired ends), still be unintended.

145

uncommitted to waking R is quite compatible with S's expecting and desiring to wake R.

The anomic sufficient conditions we have given for explanations of actions in terms of antecedent reasons allow the possibility that the very same antecedent state of the world could afford a reasons explanation for either of two or more different alternative actions. Suppose, for example, that there have been two different occasions when I have formed the intention to produce an asterisk on my computer screen and have known that either of two keys will do the job. If on one of those occasions I pressed one of those keys, my action can be explained by saying that I pressed that key in order to produce an asterisk; and if on the other occasion I pressed the other key, that action can be explained by saying that I pressed *that* key in order to produce an asterisk. The only differences we need to suppose in the two situations are in the action explained (my pressing one key rather than the other) and its concurrent intention (which I could have expressed as "By pressing *this* key, I intend to produce an asterisk"). We need suppose no differences at all in the relevant *antecedent* intention. On both occasions, it was just an intention to produce an asterisk.

In that example, the agent was indifferent between the alternative means to an intended end. In another sort of example, the agent chooses arbitrarily between incompatible desired ends. Suppose that S desires the motion to pass and at the same time desires to avoid offending her friend, who opposes the motion. Whether she votes for the motion or votes against it, the explanation can be that S did it in order to satisfy the relevant prior desire. Again, the only differences in the two alternative situations that we need to suppose, in order to make the alternative explanations hold in them, are differences in the actions and their concurrent accompaniments. We need suppose no difference in the antecedents.

Here we have a striking difference between the anomic explanatory connection we have found in explanations of actions in terms of antecedent reasons and the nomic explanatory connection in deterministic explanations of events. The nomic, deterministic connection, by its very nature, can go from a given antecedent state of the world to just one subsequent development. If the antecedent state of the world explains a subsequent development via general laws of nature, then that same antecedent state could not likewise explain any alternative development. Given fixed laws of nature, a given antecedent situation has the potential to explain nomically and deterministically at most one of the logically possible alternative developments. But the same antecedent state can explain in the anomic, reasons way any of several alternative possible subsequent actions. If the antecedent situation contains the agent's having a desire for each of two or more incompatible ends or her being indifferent between alternative means to an intended end, then it has the potential to explain in the reasons way whichever of the alternative actions occurs. The one that occurs need only have the right sort of concurrent memory and intention.[22]

It is true, as we noted earlier, that when an agent chooses arbitrarily between incompatible ends or between alternative means to

22 We have here a solution to another puzzle of van Inwagen's: one concerning how an agent can have a choice about, can have it in her power to determine, which of competing antecedent motives will cause her action, be the reason for which she acts. He expresses this puzzle in a footnote appended to his remarks I quoted earlier (in the section "The Argument from 'Undetermined' to 'Not in the Agent's Control' "):

Alvin Plantinga has suggested to me that the thief may have had a choice about whether to repent owing to his having had a choice about whether, on the one hand, *DB* [a certain complex of desire and belief in the thief] caused *R* [the thief's repenting], or, on the other, his desire for money and his belief that the poor-box contained money (*DB★*) jointly caused the event *his robbing the poor-box* (*R★*). We should note that the two desire–belief pairs, *DB* and *DB★*, both actually obtained; according to the theory Plantinga has proposed, what the thief had a choice about was which of these two potential causes became the actual cause of an effect appropriate to it. This may for all I know be the correct account of the "inner state" of a deliberating agent who has a choice about how he is going to act. But if this account is correct, then there are two events *its coming to pass that DB causes R* and *its coming to pass that DB★ causes R★* such that, though one of them must happen, it's causally undetermined which will happen; and it will have to be the case that the thief has a choice about which of them will happen. If this were so, I should find it very puzzling and I should be at a loss to give an account of it. (van Inwagen (1983), p. 239, n. 34)

The proper account seems to me straightforward. The thief determines which of the antecedent motives he acts out of simply by acting in the way recommended by one of them while concurrently remembering the motive and intending his action to satisfy it. His doing so is obviously compatible with his action's being nomically undetermined by the antecedent state of the world.

147

an intended end, we do not have an explanation of why the agent acted as she did *rather than* in one of the other ways. Nevertheless, we do have an explanation of why the agent acted as she did: She so acted in order to carry out the intention or to satisfy the relevant desire. The truth of that explanation is not undermined by the agent's not having any reason for, there not being any explanation of, her not doing one of the other things instead.

AN ANOMIC SUFFICIENT CONDITION
FOR A REASONS EXPLANATION OF
WHY THAT ACTION *RATHER THAN ANY OTHER*

But now one may wonder about cases where the antecedents explain an action in the reasons sort of way but do *not* have the potential to explain alternative actions equally well, where the antecedents give the agent's reason for acting as she did and also explain why she did not act in any alternative way instead. If such explanations must be nomic, must imply that sufficiently similar antecedents will (as a matter of the laws of nature) always lead to the same sort of action rather than to any alternative, then incompatibilism is still in serious trouble. For it would be absurd to say that any such reasons explanation of an action renders it unfree.

Incompatibilists need not worry. Such explanations need not be nomic either. Consider again reasons explanations of sort (3).

(3)   *S V*-ed in order to carry out her intention to *U*.

Our anomic sufficient condition for such an explanation was (C3).

(C3)   (a) Prior to *V*-ing, *S* had the intention to *U*, and (b) concurrently with *V*-ing, *S* remembered her prior intention and its content and intended that by this *V*-ing she would carry it out.

What sort of enriched condition will be sufficient for the truth of a similar explanation of why *S V*-ed *and* did not do something else instead (either some other sort of action or being inactive)? A commonly occurring condition that accomplishes this is the following:

(C3*)   (a) Just before *V*-ing the agent intended to *U* at once, and preferred *V*-ing then to any alternative means to *U*-ing then that occurred to her that she thought she could then perform, and (b) concurrently with *V*-ing, she remembered her prior intention and intended by this *V*-ing to carry it out, and she continued to prefer *V*-ing to any alternative means of *U*-ing that occurred to her that she thought she could then perform.

148

It is obvious that (C3*) is sufficient for the truth of a reasons explanation of the sort under consideration, one of the following form:

(3*)   S V-ed then, rather than doing something else or being inactive instead, because she intended to U at once, and she preferred V-ing to any other means of U-ing that occurred to her that she thought she could then perform.

It should be equally obvious that (C3*) does not entail that S's V-ing was nomically necessitated by its antecedents. There certainly is no plausibility in the proposition that the antecedents given in (C3*a) must always issue in S's V-ing. Often enough, such antecedents are followed by S's doing something else instead, owing to some new alternative occurring to S at the last moment, or to S's changing her mind about what alternatives are open to her, or to S's deciding to consider before acting whether she has overlooked an alternative open to her that might be preferable, or to S's suddenly abandoning (or perhaps even forgetting) her intention to U at once, or to S's weakness of will (though S believed that V-ing was definitely the best means to U-ing and therefore intended to take that means, some other means offered a temptation that she failed in the end to resist). As with the antecedents that explain why S V-ed (those given in [C3a]), the antecedents that explain why not any other alternative instead (added in [C3*a]) do so completely only in conjunction with conditions concurrent with and not antecedent to the action explained (specified in [C3*b]). To suppose that there occurs another case where the antecedents are exactly the same but where S does not V, but is inactive or does something else instead, is not to suppose anything incompatible with the truth of the explanation entailed by (C3*).

CONCLUSION

I hope to have made it clear that incompatibilism does not entail certain absurdities that it has been alleged to entail. The thesis that a free action cannot be nomically determined by its antecedents does not entail that an agent cannot determine which free action she performs or that an agent cannot perform a free action for reasons. When one sees how easy it is to give anomic sufficient conditions for reasons explanations of actions, one may find it surprising that many philosophers should have subscribed to the assumption that such explanations must be nomic. (Even some incompatibilists have been guilty of this assumption; they have typically also been "hard" determinists, denying that we in fact have free will.[23]) Perhaps the error is less surprising if we see it as a case of overgeneralizing a well-understood and highly respected paradigm, in this case the explanatory paradigm of the natural sciences where laws of nature are what make explanatory connections. Fascination with this paradigm can, it seems, blind one to the fact that the explanatory paradigm of our ordinary reasons explanations of action is quite different. There an internal and referential relation is sufficient to make the explanatory connection and has no need of a nomic connection. Neither does it rule out a nomic connection. Reasons explanations are not *in*deterministic, only *a*deterministic; but that is all that the defense of incompatibilism requires.

23 For example, Holbach (1770, chs. XI and XII), Ree (1885, chs. I and II), and Darrow (1922).

References

Adams, Marilyn McCord (1967). "Is the Existence of God a Hard Fact?",
    Philosophical Review 74, 492–503.
Anscombe, G. E. M. (1958). *Intention*. Oxford: Basil Blackwell.
Ayer, A. J. (1946). "Freedom and Necessity," *Polemic* 5; reprinted in Ayer
    (1959), 271–84.
    (1959). *Philosophical Essays*. London: Macmillan.
Bennett, Jonathan (1973). "Shooting, Killing and Dying," *Canadian Journal
    of Philosophy* 2, 315–23.
    (1984). "Counterfactuals and Temporal Direction," *Philosophical Review*
    93, 57–91.
Bergmann, Frithjof (1977). *On Being Free*. Notre Dame: University of
    Notre Dame Press.
Binkley, R., Bronaugh, R., and Marras, A., eds. (1971). *Agent, Action, and
    Reason*. Toronto: University of Toronto Press.
Brand, M., and Walton, D., eds. (1976). *Action Theory*. Dordrecht:
    D. Reidel.
Bratman, Michael (1984). "Two Faces of Intention," *Philosophical Review* 93,
    375–405.
    (1987). *Intentions, Plans, and Practical Reason*. Cambridge, MA: Harvard
    University Press.
Broad, C. D. (1952). *Ethics and the History of Philosophy*. London: Routledge
    & Kegan Paul.
Chisholm, Roderick M. (1966). "Freedom and Action," in Lehrer, ed.
    (1966), 11–44.
    (1976a). "The Agent as Cause," in Brand and Walton, eds. (1976), 199–
    211.
    (1976b). *Person and Object*. London: George Allen & Unwin.
D'Arcy, Eric (1963). *Human Acts*. Oxford: Clarendon Press.
Darrow, Clarence (1922). *Crime, Its Cause and Treatment*. New York: Crow-
    ell.
Davidson, Donald (1963). "Actions, Reasons, and Causes," *Journal of Phi-
    losophy* 60, 685–700; reprinted in Davidson (1980), 3–19.
    (1967). "The Logical Form of Action Sentences," in Rescher, ed. (1967),
    81–95; reprinted in Davidson (1980), 105–22.
    (1970). "Mental Events," in Foster and Swanson, eds. (1970); reprinted
    in Davidson (1980), 207–25.
    (1971). "Agency," in Binkley, Bronaugh, and Marras, eds. (1971), 3–25;
    reprinted in Davidson (1980), 43–61.

(1980). *Essays on Actions and Events.* Oxford: Clarendon Press.

Davis, Lawrence H. (1970). "Individuation of Actions," *Journal of Philosophy* 67, 520–30.

(1979). *Theory of Action.* Englewood Cliffs, NJ: Prentice-Hall.

Dennett, Daniel C. (1984). *Elbow Room: Varieties of Free Will Worth Wanting.* Cambridge, MA: MIT Press.

Dworkin, Gerald, ed. (1970). *Determinism, Free Will, and Moral Responsibility.* Englewood Cliffs, NJ: Prentice-Hall.

Eccles, J. C. (1953). *The Neurophysiological Basis of Mind.* Oxford: Oxford University Press.

(1970). *Facing Reality.* London: English University Press.

Edwards, Paul, and Pap, Arthur, eds. (1973). *A Modern Introduction to Philosophy.* New York: Free Press.

Fischer, John Martin (1982). "Responsibility and Control," *Journal of Philosophy* 89, 24–40; reprinted in Fischer, ed. (1986b), 174–90.

(1983a). "Freedom and Foreknowledge," *Philosophical Review* 92, 67–79.

(1983b). "Incompatibilism," *Philosophical Studies* 43, 127–37.

(1985). "Ockhamism," *Philosophical Review* 94, 80–100.

(1986a). "Hard-Type Soft Facts," *Philosophical Review* 95, 591–601.

ed. (1986b). *Moral Responsibility.* Ithaca, NY: Cornell University Press.

(1988). "Freedom and Miracles," *Nous* 22, 235–52.

Foster, L., and Swanson, J., eds. (1970). *Experience and Theory.* London: Duckworth.

Frankfurt, Harry (1969). "Alternate Possibilities and Moral Responsibility," *Journal of Philosophy* 66, 828–39.

(1971). "Freedom of the Will and the Concept of a Person," *Journal of Philosophy* 68, 5–20.

Ginet, Carl (1966). "Might We Have No Choice?" in Lehrer, ed. (1966), 87–104.

(1975). *Knowledge, Perception, and Memory.* Dordrecht: D. Reidel.

(1980). "The Conditional Analysis of Freedom," in van Inwagen, ed. (1980), 171–86.

(1983). "In Defense of Incompatibilism," *Philosophical Studies* 44, 391–400.

Goldman, Alvin I. (1969). "The Compatibility of Mechanism and Purpose," *Philosophical Review* 78, 468–82.

(1970). *A Theory of Human Action.* Englewood Cliffs, NJ: Prentice-Hall.

(1971). "The Individuation of Action," *Journal of Philosophy* 68, 761–74.

(1976). "The Volitional Theory Revisited," in Brand and Walton, eds. (1976), 67–85.

Harman, Gilbert (1976). "Practical Reasoning," *Review of Metaphysics* 29, 431–63.

Hart, H. L. A., and Honore, A. M. (1959). *Causation in the Law.* Oxford: Clarendon Press.

Hoffman, Joshua (1979). "Pike on Possible Worlds, Divine Foreknowledge, and Human Freedom," *Philosophical Review* 88, 433–42.

Hoffman, Joshua, and Rosenkrantz, Gary (1984). "Hard and Soft Facts," *Philosophical Review* 93, 419–34.

Holbach, Paul Henri Thiry, Baron d' (1770). *Système de la Nature*, English translation, *System of Nature* (1808). Philadelphia: R. T. Rawl.

Hornsby, Jennifer (1980). *Actions*. London: Routledge & Kegan Paul.

Kim, Jaegwon (1966). "On the Psycho-Physical Identity Theory," *American Philosophical Quarterly* 3, 227–35.

Lehrer, Keith, ed. (1966). *Freedom and Determinism*. New York: Random House.

Lewis, David (1981). "Are We Free to Break the Laws?" *Theoria* 47, 112–21.

Malcolm, Norman (1968). "The Conceivability of Mechanism," *Philosophical Review* 77, 45–72.

Melden, A. I. (1961). *Free Action*. London: Routledge & Kegan Paul.

Mill, John Stuart (1872). *An Examination of Sir William Hamilton's Philosophy*, ed. J. M. Robson (1979). Toronto: University of Toronto Press.

Pike, Nelson (1966). "Of God and Freedom: A Rejoinder," *Philosophical Review* 75, 369–79.

(1977). "Divine Foreknowledge, Human Freedom, and Possible Worlds," *Philosophical Review* 86, 209–16.

Prichard, H. A. (1949). *Moral Obligation*. Oxford: Clarendon Press.

Ree, Paul (1885). *Die Illusion der Willens Freiheit*. Most of Chapters 1 and 2, translated by Stefan Bauer-Mengelberg under the title "Determinism and the Illusion of Moral Responsibility," appear in Edwards and Pap, eds. (1973), 10–27.

Reid, Thomas (1815). *The Works of Thomas Reid*, Vols. III and IV. Charlestown, MA: Samuel Etheridge, Jr.

Rescher, Nicholas, ed. (1967). *The Logic of Decision and Action*. Pittsburgh: University of Pittsburgh Press.

Saunders, John Turk (1966). "Of God and Freedom," *Philosophical Review* 75, 219–25.

Searle, John (1970). *Speech Acts*. Cambridge: Cambridge University Press.

(1983). *Intentionality*. Cambridge: Cambridge University Press.

(1984). *Minds, Brains, and Science*. London: British Broadcasting Corporation.

Sellars, Wilfrid (1976). "Volitions Re-affirmed," in Brand and Walton, eds. (1976), 47–66.

Shwayder, David S. (1965). *The Stratification of Behavior*. New York: Humanities Press.

Sidgwick, Henry (1907). *The Methods of Ethics*, 7th ed. London: Macmillan.

Slote, Michael (1982). "Selective Necessity and the Free Will Problem," *Journal of Philosophy* 79, 5–24.

Smart, J. J. C. (1968). *Between Science and Philosophy*. New York: Random House.

Taylor, Richard (1966). *Action and Purpose*. Englewood Cliffs, NJ: Prentice-Hall.

Thomson, Judith J. (1971a). "The Time of a Killing," *Journal of Philosophy* 68, 115–32.

(1971b). "Individuating Actions," *Journal of Philosophy* 68, 774–81.

(1977). *Acts and Other Events*. Ithaca, NY: Cornell University Press.

153

Thorp, John (1980). *Free Will: A Defense Against Neuro-Physiological Determinism*. London: Routledge & Kegan Paul.

van Inwagen, Peter (1974). "A Formal Approach to the Problem of Free Will and Determinism," *Theoria* 40, 9–22.

(1975). "The Incompatibility of Free Will and Determinism," *Philosophical Studies* 27, 185–99.

ed. (1980). *Time and Cause: Essays Presented to Richard Taylor*. Dordrecht: D. Reidel.

(1983). *An Essay on Free Will*. Oxford: Clarendon Press.

Watson, Gary (1975). "Free Agency," *Journal of Philosophy* 72, 205–20.

ed. (1982). *Free Will*. Oxford: Oxford University Press.

Widerker, David (1987). "On an Argument for Incompatibilism," *Analysis* 47, 37–41.

Wilson, George (1980). *The Intentionality of Human Action*. Amsterdam: North-Holland.

Wittgenstein, Ludwig (1958). *Philosophical Investigations*, 3rd ed. Oxford: Basil Blackwell.

Zimmerman, Michael J. (1984). *An Essay on Human Action*. New York: Peter Lang.

Index

absentminded action, 88–9
abstract event/action, 57
act-token, 48
action designator, 18–19, 45–6, 51, 58, 62; co-agential, 65, 67; co-temporal, 65, 67
action tree, 46–8, 73
action type, 45–6, 48
actish phenomenal quality, x, 11, 13–15, 20, 22, 25
Adams, M., 102
addict, 118; unwilling, 121; willing, 121
adeterministic, *see* anomic sufficient condition for reasons explanation
afferent neural capacity, 29
agent-causation, 8, 12–14
agent(s), ix, 3–4, 8, 12–13, 16, 20, 23–5, 47–51, 56, 73–4, 76–7, 80, 84, 88–9, 92, 95–8, 101–2, 105–6, 108, 114–18, 121, 124–31, 134–5, 138–49
aggregate action (conjunction of actions), 19–20, 49, 65–6, 73, 117; intentionality of, 86–7, and belief about components, 87
aiming an action at something, 77
alternative actions, x, 90
angle brackets, 2
anomic sufficient condition for reasons explanation, 124, 136–7, 146, 149; in terms of antecedent desire, 4, 143, 145; in terms of antecedent intention, 4, 142; in terms of concurrent intention, 138, 141; of why that action rather than any other, 148–9
Anscombe, E., 16, 47, 70
antecedent desire, 4, 139, 143
antecedent intention, 4, 139–41, 143, 146
arbitrary choice, 135, 147
Audi, R., x, xi
avoiding, 21–2
Ayer, A. J., 129

backtracking compatibilist, 107–10
backtracking incompatibilist, 111
backtracking view of counterfactuals, 107, 110
backward causation, 105
bare opportunities, 96
basic action, 15, 20, 49, 70, 73, 75, 117; designator, 18, 20, 49, 63–4; type, 121–2
behaviorism, philosophical, 24
belief, ix, 3; about how and intentional action, 79–80, 85, 87
Bell inequalities, 93
Belzer, M., xi
Bennett, D., 78
Bennett, John, xi
Bennett, Jonathan, 62, 107
Bergmann, F., 125, 130
blind nature, 117
bodily part: in action, 67; and volitional content, 36–7, 40–2
brain process specific to voluntary exertion, 8–11, 20, 138, 144
Bratman, M., xi, 32, 75–6, 137, 145
Broad, C. D., 13–14
Bromberger, S., xi
"by", 16–17, 58; contrasted with "in", 17; with exemplifyings of properties expresses composition or supervenience, 58
BY relation, 18–19, 46–7, 53–4, 63, 66, 68–70; antisymmetrical, 53; argument from, 53–4

canonical event/action designators, 1–2, 18–19, 45–6, 52, 65–7, 73, 99
Cartesian dualism, 93
causal explanations, 141
causal-explanatory relations, 69; argument from, 53–8; between exemplifyings of properties, 55–6
causal generation, 15, 18

155

higher order volitions, 120
Hoffman, J., 102–3
Holbach, P. H. T., Baron d', 150
Honore, A. M., 6
Hornsby, J., 15, 29, 34, 47, 60–1, 70
Hughes, C., xi, 7, 10
Hume, D., 124

illusion of voluntary exertion, 39
impression of freedom, 90, 93, 116;
    inescapability of, 91
incompatibilism, x, Ch. 5 passim, 124,
    126, 129, 148–9; argument for stated,
    106; defined, 97
inconsistent intentions and absent-
    minded action, 88–9
indeterminacy, 125–6
indeterministic processes, 93
indifferent means, 135
individuation of action, x, Ch. 3 passim
inescapability of the laws, principle of,
    105–6, 111–16
"in order to", 137–8, 141–3
instability of mismatch between voli-
    tional contents and effects, 42
instrument in action, 67–8
intention, 3, 33, 51; to exert, 43–4;
    occurrent, 32
intentional action, x, Ch. 4 passim
intentional exertion, 43
intentional under designator, 72
intention in action, 36
internal relation in reasons explanation,
    141, 150
intrinsic account of action, 3–4
intrinsically intentional action, 74
intrinsic/internal features of an action,
    51, 66–8
introspectionist psychology, 24
inverting spectacles, 44
involuntary, 8, 23, 29
involuntary exertion, 5
irresistible craving, 118, 120–1

James, W., 37
justification of belief about how, and
    intentional action, 80–7; and memory
    lapse, 85–7

Kim, J., 48
kinesthetic images, 37–8
kinesthetic perception, 28, 37–8, 41,
    43–4

knowledge, ix

law* of nature, 105
law** of nature, 105
laws of nature, 92, 94–5, 105, 107, 110,
    134, 140; and explanatory paradigm
    of natural sciences, 150
layered structure of complex actions,
    50–1, 65, 74
Lewis, D., 107, 112–13
Local Miracle compatibilist, 111–12
Local Miracle view of counterfactuals,
    107, 111
luck: and an action's being open to
    agent, 96–7; and intentional action,
    78, 80

making it the case that p, 100–1, 113;
    defined, 98–9; where p is univer-
    sal generalization or negation of
    universal generalization, 100–1
Malcolm, N., 136
manipulation, 116, 138, 144
manner of action, 67–8
match-ensuring mechanism in volun-
    tary exertion, 40–2
materialist and volition, 31
maximizing view on individuation of
    actions, 47, 53, 70
Melden, A. I., 136
mental saying, 12–13, 23, 73
metaphysical, ix
method in action, 67–8
middle view on individuation of
    actions, 48–50, 70
Mill, J. S., 131–5
Mill's law, 132–3
minimally sufficient condition, 100;
    defined, 99
minimizing view on individuation of
    actions, 47, 49, 53, 59, 70
modus ponens for power necessity, 104
moral antecedents, 131, 134
morality, ix
moral responsibility, 93, 126
motives, 119–20

Nefarious Neurosurgeon, The, 116
negated action designator, 21
negative action, 1
neutral designator, 72, 74–5
New York Times, 100

157

nomic explanation/connection, 135, 140, 144, 146, 150; in reasons explanation of action, 136, 142, 148–9
nomic necessitation of action, 124, 127, 136–7, 140–1; through its motives, 115
nonaction, 1; part of actions, 64
nonbasic action, 16, 74, 117, *see also* complex action; designator, 49

Occam's razor, 64
ontological parsimony, 64, 70
open alternatives, x, 90, 116, 127
open possibility of a proposition, 101–2, 105–6, 117, 122; contrasted with logical possibility, 101, 104
open to an agent: to make it the case that *p*, 101–2, 115, 117, 121–3, *see also* open possibility of a proposition; to perform action, 95, 101, 102, 105, 117, 127, broader and narrower notions of, 96–7; to perform basic action, 118–23
overdetermination, 100

Peirce, C. S., 24
personal events and states, ix, 1, 45
physical determinism, 92–3
Pike, N., 102–3
planning, 76, 145; contrasted with execution, 11, 33
Plantinga, A., 147
power necessity, 104
prevailing motive, 132–4
Prichard, H. A., 15, 29, 34
prudential, ix
psychological determinism, 92–3
psychophysical laws, 93

quantum theory, 93–4
Quine, W. V. O., 2

random event, 129–31, 136
Raskolnikov, 125–6
"rather than", 135, 148–9
rational agency and persons, 4
rationality, ix
reasons explanation of action, x, 3–4, 70, Ch. 6 passim; adeterministic, not indeterministic, 150
Ree, P., 150
refraining, 22
regress, unacceptable, 7–8

Reid, T., 132–4
remembering, anomic sufficient condition for, 144
representational account of volitional content, 37
responsibility (credit) and intentional action, 76, 80, 84
responsible action, 130
result of action as part of larger action, 49–52, 58–9, 63, 65, 73–5
robot, 20
Rosencrantz, G., 102

Saunders, J. T., 102
Searle, J., 29, 36, 91
seeming to remember, default explanation of, 144
self-deception, 121
self-reference: in the content of intention, 35–6; in the content of volition, 35
Sellars, W., 32, 34
sense experience in perception, 24
Shwayder, D., 47
side effect of an action, 145
Sidgwick, H., 76
simple mental action, 11–15, 20, 30, 49–50, 65, 73–5, 94, 118
Slote, M., 115
Smart, J. J. C., 129, 136
Socrates, ix
spontaneous action, 3, 130, 140
strongest motive, 132, 134; and pleasure and pain, 133
strongest motive law, 133–4
surprise and volitional content, 38, 43

Taylor, R., 4, 7
temporal relations, argument from, 53, 58–63
Thomson, J., 2, 4, 48, 53, 58, 62
Thorp, J., 62, 94
Tomberlin, J., x
trying, 9, 10; distinguished from trying to act, 10; to exert, 30–1, 43

unavoidability, 115–16, 120
undetermined event/action, 124–8

van Iwagen, P., xi, 95, 97, 103, 112, 126, 128, 147
Vihvelin, K., xi

volition, x, Ch. 2 passim, 9, 12, 15, 49, 73, 75, 92, 131, 144; content of tied to immediate present, 32–3; correlation with (dependence on) neural process, 8–11, 20, 92, 94; as part of voluntary exertion, 29, 33, 39, 49–51, 117

voluntariness of experience of voluntary exertion, 28

voluntary, 8, 23; experiencing exertion as, 24, 27

voluntary control, 40; direct vs. indirect, 34.

voluntary exertion, ix–x, Ch. 2 passim, 8–11, 20, 50–1, 73, 117, 138; awareness of, 24–7, in vocalizing, 26–7

Washington Post, 100

Watson, G., 120

wayward causal chains, 78–9

weakness of will, 120

Widerker, D., xi, 68, 74, 104

willing, 12; stipulated notion of, 31–2; *see also* volition

Wilson, G., 84–5, 139

Wittgenstein, L., 24

Zimmerman, M., 4, 10, 34

159